# Information Governance and Security

# Information Governance and Security

## Protecting and Managing Your Company's Proprietary Information

John G. Iannarelli
Michael O'Shaughnessy

AMSTERDAM • BOSTON • HEIDELBERG • LONDON
NEW YORK • OXFORD • PARIS • SAN DIEGO
SAN FRANCISCO • SINGAPORE • SYDNEY • TOKYO
Butterworth-Heinemann is an imprint of Elsevier

Acquiring Editor: Brian Romer
Editorial Project Manager: Keira Bunn
Project Manager: Priya Kumaraguruparan
Designer: Alan Studholme

Butterworth Heinemann is an imprint of Elsevier
The Boulevard, Langford Lane, Kidlington, Oxford OX5 1GB, UK
225 Wyman Street, Waltham, MA 02451, USA

**Notices**

Knowledge and best practice in this field are constantly changing. As new research and experience broaden
our understanding, changes in research methods or professional practices, may become necessary.

Practitioners and researchers must always rely on their own experience and knowledge in evaluating and
using any information or methods described herein. In using such information or methods they should
be mindful of their own safety and the safety of others, including parties for whom they have a professional responsibility.

To the fullest extent of the law, neither the Publisher nor the authors, contributors, or editors, assume any
liability for any injury and/or damage to persons or property as a matter of products liability, negligence
or otherwise, or from any use or operation of any methods, products, instructions, or ideas contained in
the material herein.

**Library of Congress Cataloging-in-Publication Data**
Iannarelli, John.
  Information governance and security : protecting and managing your company's
proprietary information / John Iannarelli, Michael O'Shaughnessy.
    pages cm
  Includes index.
1. Knowledge management. I. O'Shaughnessy, Michael. II. Title.
HD30.2.I2336 2014
658.4'038--dc23

                         2014027431

**British Library Cataloging-in-Publication Data**
A catalogue record for this book is available from the British Library

ISBN: 978-0-12-800247-6

For information on all Butterworth-Heinemann publications
visit our website at http://store.elsevier.com/

Working together
to grow libraries in
developing countries

www.elsevier.com • www.bookaid.org

# Dedication

*To the men and women of the FBI, the finest law enforcement agency in the world.*
John G. Iannarelli

*To my wife, Karen, for all of your love and support.*
Michael O'Shaughnessy

# Contents

# About the Authors

**John G. Iannarelli** has been an agent with the Federal Bureau of Investigation for twenty years, specializing in cyber investigations. He has been assigned to Detroit, San Diego, Washington, and Phoenix, where he currently serves as the assistant special agent in charge, the FBI's number two position in Arizona.

In 2012, Mr. Iannarelli received an honorary doctorate of computer science for his contributions to the field of cyber investigations. He has presented at national and international gatherings, including presentations to Fortune 500 companies, law enforcement agencies, and the Vatican. He is the author of several books, including his recently released *Why Teens Fail and What to Fix*, a guide to protecting children from Internet dangers.

Previously Mr. Iannarelli served as a San Diego police officer. He is an attorney admitted to the bars of California, Maryland, and the District of Columbia.

Since 2009, **Michael O'Shaughnessy** has served as the president of Guardian Pro, a collaboration of highly qualified and uniquely experienced individuals dedicated to the mission of protecting the private sector. As the founder of Guardian Pro, Mr. O'Shaughnessy brings a heavy technical and security background and the vision to grow a company focused on educating the public and corporations, and changing the landscape of technical security awareness and knowledge.

Prior to Guardian Pro, he worked at a computer forensics company from 2004 to 2009. There he oversaw the growth of the company from 10 to 108 employees and saw revenues increase from 2 million to more than 24 million dollars. The company expanded services outside of forensics to include consulting, litigation support, and electronic discovery.

He began his career with United Airlines and spent eighteen years in operational, strategic, and security management. He served as international manager at Chicago and Miami, operations chief in Chicago, and security manager at Washington, DC, and Glasgow, Scotland, as well as general manager in Utah and Arizona.

# Survey and Disclaimer

Unless otherwise noted, all comments offered by business representatives in this book are based on responses to an October 2013 information governance survey conducted by the authors. Fifty individuals representing small, medium, and large businesses throughout the United States responded to the survey.

Although John G. Iannarelli is a special agent with the Federal Bureau of Investigation (FBI), this work is based solely on the authors' own views and research, and does not in any way represent the official position of the FBI. Any references to the FBI are the result of the authors' research and have been adapted from public sources.

# Foreword

Toward the end of my thirty-year career in law enforcement, I served as the assistant director of the Federal Bureau of Investigation's (FBI) Cyber Division, overseeing criminal cyber investigations worldwide. After retiring from the FBI, I have subsequently served as the director of security for two major corporations with responsibility for thousands of employees, hundreds of facilities, and numerous sophisticated technologies. In my professional experience—having been witness to more losses of proprietary and personal information than I could possibly count—one of the common themes in each of these incidents was the failure to have an adequate information governance plan to guard against and mitigate such incidents.

For most companies and individuals, protecting against the loss of proprietary and personal information is nothing more than ensuring that a firewall is in place. Sadly though, this does little to protect against today's threats to information security. Individuals and companies alike need to be proactive against the growing threats and need to take their information governance planning seriously. It appears that everyone is aware of the potential for a computer intrusion, but little efforts are directed toward any of the threats from within, whether they are nefarious or unintentional.

I have seen significant losses of proprietary and personal information, not just from the criminal intrusion but from the well-meaning employee who compromises operations by being socially engineered. Likewise, there are the disgruntled workers who choose to take their frustrations out on the company by means of sabotage. In any of these cases, much of the damage could have been prevented, or at the very least minimized, had a proper information governance policy been incorporated into everyday functions.

I have had the pleasure of working directly with both authors of this book, and can think of no other persons better suited to explore comprehensively and explain the threats and the solutions through information governance planning. Their combined law enforcement and corporate experiences make them exceptionally well suited to share their experiences while imparting their unique knowledge of implementing policies and practices designed to keep you and your business safe.

Whether you are the sole proprietor of a small operation, or the chief information officer of a major conglomerate, within these pages you will find a takeaway to minimize and potentially prevent the potential—or shall I say inevitable—loss of sensitive data. For as the authors will tell you, it is not a matter of if but rather when you become a victim in today's world of handling sensitive information.

**Jana D. Monroe**
*Former Assistant Director Cyber Division*
*Federal Bureau of Investigation*

*You are the primary victims of the evolving cyberthreat. But you are also the key to defeating it. You have the information on your servers and your networks. And you have the expertise and the knowledge we need to stop these attacks. You need zealously to guard your proprietary information and your customer data.*

**James Comey**
Federal Bureau of Investigation Director
(*Source:* from his speech in RSA Conference,
San Francisco, California, 26 February 2014)

# Chapter 1

# The Case for Information Governance

Guarding assets, staff, and accounts has always been a key to protecting businesses. But in the information age, are you protecting your most important resources— company and client data? Each year, businesses lose billions of dollars due to data leakage, on top of which the government often imposes millions in fines. In addition, leakage can cause irreparable damage to your company's reputation. It is not a matter of if you will be a victim; it is a matter of when.

We have all heard the old adage that an ounce of prevention is worth a pound of cure. When it comes to data management, that pound of cure may not be available, so the new adage might be that an ounce of prevention is worth preventing the total destruction of your business. The ounce of prevention is information governance, and—if you are like most people—you have no idea what that is or how to take advantage of it.

This book explains how you—as a business owner, executive, or even someone just interested in keeping their proprietary information safe—can better adapt to twenty-first-century threats. By understanding the changing landscape and moving your organization to be focused and data centric, the damage or loss of your key information can be minimized if not out-right prevented. We will break down for you what information governance is and does for different sized companies. Large, medium, and small companies all have unique circumstances that will be addressed. Additionally, we will discuss what they have in common. Information governance has many standard issues that can and should be addressed across all organizations.

One of the benefits of reading this book is the impact on your personal life. While this book is written to help in business, many of the tools and habits discussed are important for individuals. Digital threats affect people at work and at home. Be mindful as you read to see the parallels to your life away from the office.

Let's start with a bold statement: information governance is *not* a function of your information technology group. It is a base-level management function, much like human resources or finance. A properly developed and managed information governance program protects your company and keeps it effective and efficient. It helps to manage compliance issues and can be vital in defending against litigation. It will make employees more satisfied and secure in their work and limits your risk of loss from human error. Information governance is more than an IT problem that needs to be solved; it is a systemic solution to counteract threats, alleviate inefficiencies, and prepare for the future.

Take, for example, the story of an architectural firm located in the southwestern United States that was happily doing business as a profitable midsized company in the spring of 2011. The employees were engaged. The clients were happy. The company was making money and having a great time. All seemed well, so what could go wrong?

During that time a senior designer with full access to the client base and design work resigned and went to work for a competitor. In very short order, clients started leaving and much of the work was shifted to the competing firm by whom the employee had been hired. Not good.

In an effort to stop the bleeding, the firm's owner went to his attorney to take action on this sabotage by stopping the theft of clients and company designs. Upon review with legal counsel it was determined the employee had never been asked or required to sign a nondisclosure or a noncompete agreement. The owner even contacted law enforcement in an effort to right the wrong, but received the same response. There was nothing they could do. The former employee was not in breach of contract, nor could criminal intent be proven in a court of law.

The victim company was able to recover, but only after shrinking in size, laying off office personnel, and moving to a new, smaller building. Several years later, they have still not fully regained their previous work levels. The situation was tragic and preventable. It occurred because the architectural firm did not have a policy that addressed data management and access. They had no employee agreements to hinder or address the theft of intellectual property. They had no information governance program to steer management to avoid such problems.

## Information Governance

So what exactly do we mean when we talk about information governance? It is a set of established policies and procedures you and your employees implement and follow in order to manage sensitive and proprietary information.

For smaller businesses, which can be anything from a sole proprietor up to approximately fifty employees, participation in information governance should be from the top down. The smaller the organization, however, the more concentrated the development and implementation can be. Ensuring that everyone understands what they are supposed to do with important information and how to do it can make the difference in protecting the company's vital interests. This understanding evolves as the threats and benefits of the digital age become clearer. Likewise, information governance can be applied in such a fashion that the company's performance improves, productivity increases, and employee satisfaction can be positively impacted.

So does the small business need to be concerned with taking the same actions as the big guys on the block? Absolutely! Loss and compromise of important information knows no boundaries. Small businesses are just as susceptible to threats, whether it is inadvertent yet preventable damage to proprietary information or the nefarious actions of some individuals interested in disrupting operations. But even if a lone employee operates the small business, that person needs to be just as vigilant in following the proper procedures to protect the company's interests. In some instances, a small yet successful business is a greater target, as it may appear less diligent and secure than a larger organization.

A medium-size company (50–1,500 employees) will have the same interests, yet based on its size, there may be fewer levels. Officers in the company will likely have multiple roles and broader discretion in implementing procedures, along with the ability to change those procedures as the need arises. Most medium-sized enterprises drive decisions to lower levels, which in effect makes an information governance program and its corresponding communication mechanisms even more important.

For large businesses (over 2,500 employees), participation by personnel would incorporate all facets of the company, from the CEO down to the front-line employee.

## The Small Business

In many small businesses, just one person is in charge. The owner is responsible for everything, be it marketing, sales, operations, finance, or strategy. The dilemma facing most small business owners is staying on top of all of the details while keeping the business profitable. Small business owners have enough to worry about without having what they might perceive as unnecessary responsibilities placed upon them. The case for information governance, however, is much like purchasing insurance. Policyholders hope never to use the insurance, but they understand the risk and plan accordingly.

A Ponemon–Experian cyber insurance study determined that nearly 20 percent of all cyber attacks are specifically aimed at businesses with 250 or fewer employees.[1] For a small business, information governance is just another layer of insurance, but one that is more likely than not to be put into use. The results of not having an information governance program can be devastating for a small business.

An excellent example of a small business that needed a solid information governance policy is a real estate investment company owned by Jeff. Jeff has a thriving business. He makes a nice living and enjoys what he does. His six employees seem to be satisfied and everyone works well together. Everything appears to be fine. Yet as the company clicks along, a danger hides within the work force. A trusted employee is harboring ill will and thinks he can do what Jeff does—and profit like Jeff does. But whereas Jeff built his company over time from the ground up, the nefarious employee is looking for a quicker way to make money.

Initially, the employee adds some items to his expense reports, but soon moves to demanding—and getting—kickbacks from contractors. Eventually, this hidden threat finds a way to skim profit off the sale of properties, too. His actions go unnoticed by Jeff, who has nothing in place to check on the integrity of employees or to verify the financials being reported. Jeff is a victim and does not know it. He has no system to identify the issue. He just notices his numbers getting slightly worse over time.

This is a sad but common issue with small business. The owner is too tied up in the minutia to see the real problem, and his lack of planning and adherence to a set of rules and policies has hindered his ability to protect his organization. A solid, yet manageable information governance program would have—at the very least—given the owner a more direct path to determining the problem, At its best, such governance could have weeded out a potential problem before any damage was done.

## CLIENTS

Clients are the lifeblood of a small business operation. The loss of a single client could have a serious financial impact on the company. Even more significantly, damage caused to the client's vital information will also result in the loss of future income from this particular client. The reputation damage the business sustains as a result of this loss is likely to impact the status of other clients. It is clear that companies see cyber security threats as a significant liability, and we are seeing increased interest from customers in managing against this risk. Why would customers knowingly choose to do business with your company if you cannot guarantee the security of their important information?

Obviously all clients are valued, but ask yourself these questions:

1. Are we treating the client's data as we would want our data to be treated? Are we keeping it safe and secure? Just as importantly, are we handling it efficiently?
2. Are we doing what we can with our own information to serve them better?
3. Are the clients handling their own data in a way that minimizes our risks? Are they secure? If not, could it impact our information or that of our other clients?

If you answered no to any of these questions, the solution lies in how you administer your information and that of your clients. If the problem resides with the client, it is incumbent upon you to change and adapt while working with them to improve their processes.

## EMPLOYEES

One of the main sources of information loss in a small business is the company's own employees. Sometimes it is simply the negligent handling of information by an employee who has not been properly educated about the threats and how to prevent against loss. That is easily fixed through education and training.

Unfortunately, the unintentional mishandling of information is not the only threat. Just as likely is the nefarious employee who purposefully damages the business's operation for any number of reasons. In an informal conversation in early 2013, Mark Pribish, Director of Customer Relations for Merchants Information Solutions—a Phoenix-based corporation specializing in employee screening and credit report restoration—said that during the course of an average work history, one in eight employees will purposefully engage in an action that is hurtful to their employer. Motivations include a desire for revenge, dissatisfaction with their job, spite, and a variety of other reasons. In most cases, this negative action jeopardizes both customer relations and profitability.

For their own sanity and for the sake of the company, most small business owners must delegate large amounts of responsibility to employees. This is both a blessing and a curse. It is a blessing due to the fact that without others taking responsibility, a company can and will stagnate. Growth occurs when a team works together and the leadership is freed to develop a vision for the future and to plan for the implementation of that vision. The problems occur when individuals take advantage of that freedom and responsibility. Information governance guards against this by laying out clear policies and procedures, along with the implementation of a system of checks and balances.

Additionally, employees who work for small companies are often given more access to data than they would have at larger companies. This greater span of control gives the employee a larger window for malfeasance, manipulation, or simple mistakes. Once again, a good policy that defines access and has controls in place is vital to the security of the data.

## CONTRACTORS

From an information governance perspective, contractors and subcontractors are no different than a company's own employees. Small businesses often run on the assistance of outside help. The only difference is that employers probably know less about their contractors than they do about their employees. How are the contractors trained? Do they know and understand the threats that arise from not following good information governance practices? Do they understand their own contractor policies? We only need to look at Richard Snowden, a contractor working for the National Security Agency (NSA), who admittedly took it upon himself to release highly sensitive government data to the media. Surely both the NSA and their contractor had specific information governance policies in place, yet significant damage occurred. This relates directly to the one in eight statistic mentioned earlier. It is a pretty sure bet that if the NSA cannot fully protect their information, your information is at risk as well.

## FINDING A BALANCE

Admittedly, placing a strong emphasis on information governance can skew the balance of profitability, growth, and performance that a small business works so hard to achieve. In order to establish and maintain that balance, however, you must include having a thorough information governance plan that is on equal footing with other major disciplines such as finance, sales, and operations.

Take, for example, the medical profession. A small doctor's office has the need for a proper information governance policy just as much as a large practice, and perhaps even more so. Think about the kind of proprietary information that a medical practice retains. Even a small independent physician's office will have the medical records for each of its patients, which will include not just medical history but personal identifiers such as social security numbers and dates of birth, along with records of credit card and bank account numbers from past payments. If the information kept by a larger practice is compromised, it could be extremely costly and damaging to their reputation. The compromise of a small office's patient information could make financial recovery impossible. But these concerns are not limited to just those in a small medical office. Shop owners, landscapers, and all other types of small businesses generally maintain these sorts of personal identification records. The safety of this proprietary information is no less important to the customer, which translates into the responsibility of the business owner.

In a small business it is important to have the proper balance in order to ensure that the information governance policy is a benefit to the operation and not a hindrance. As important as it is to protecting the business, too much focus on just one area can kill creativity. Policies are no good if they are too restrictive and prevent workers from getting the job done. Striking the proper balance can make a small business more effective and more profitable by limiting the company's risk.

## The Medium Size Business

The larger the business size, the more potential issues you will encounter in securing important information. Human resources will have more employee personal information, and the company will have more employees who might mistakenly or purposefully disclose sensitive information. A good information governance plan will incorporate human resources personnel so that they may be part of the equation in safeguarding the data by hiring correctly, vetting thoroughly, and training properly the employees to do the same.

Additionally, the larger the company the more the business will attract threats from the outside. Ransom scams and spear phishing (discussed later) are on the rise, and the larger the business the more profitable these scams can be for the perpetrator. A small one-man operation may not be worth the time financially to crooks, while a larger corporation may be too difficult to penetrate. The medium size business is probably just right for such a scam.

### EMPLOYEES AND MANAGERS

As with small businesses, medium-sized companies are vulnerable to rogue or careless employees. According the Ponemon Institute, internal identity theft accounts for 73 percent of all identity theft cases in the US.[2] The statistics tell the story that employees are an enormous yet continually growing threat when it comes to data security. The process of managing in the environment of big data is daunting. As stated previously, human resources is a vital piece of the puzzle to ensure against your company's risk from within.

### BUSINESS ASSOCIATES AND PARTNERS

Business associates and partners are another reality of the business world, particularly in medium and large businesses that are seeking to manage their operational costs most effectively. The use of other companies, other departments, or outside individuals to augment operations is common and growing. A good information governance policy will help not only to manage people working for you who are not your own employees but will also mitigate any risk they can potentially bring into your business.

Many companies fail to vet, train, and verify those coming in from the outside, even when those individuals will be working with data. Think about that for a moment. You are bringing into your organization someone you have most likely never met, about whom you probably know little, and who has not been vetted, and yet you are going to give him full administrative access. This stranger now has the keys to your kingdom. Scary.

## PROFITABILITY AND BALANCE

Like the small business, the medium-size organization also needs to find the right balance between the protection of information and ensuring this protection does not hinder profitability. Striking the right balance will depend greatly on the size of the organization and ease with which rules can be implemented and adjusted. The primary focus should be on the business, but a secondary mission is ensuring that the business does not damage itself.

Russ Johnson, the President of Merchants Information Solutions, told us that information governance helps his company achieve its goals.[3] "We are an information solutions provider and by staying current with best practices it allows us to compete on a level playing field with much larger companies."

## RESPONSIBLE STEWARDSHIP

Someone has to be in charge of the information governance policies and lead the way for others in the company. In a medium-size business, there will likely be more than one person working toward this goal, but ultimately someone must be appointed to head the effort with others working in supporting roles. Identifying and empowering the necessary people are just as important as having a workable information governance plan.

No matter what the organizational size, those responsible must be recognized as clear leaders and—much like operations or finance managers—must be held accountable. The development and management of the necessary policies and procedures need to be understood at all levels so that the ideas become engrained in the culture of the business. Information governance should become a part of the fabric of the business.

Matthew Fehling, President and CEO at the Better Business Bureau of Central, Northern, and Western Arizona, described for us how information governance is facilitated in his organization.[4] "Company officers, in conjunction with the IT director, oversee the implementation of the information governance policies. All policies are reviewed bi-annually, or in some cases more frequently as needed." This is a great example for all business of how responsible stewardship should be implemented to the benefit of everyone involved.

# The Large Business

Large businesses and corporations most likely will already have some level of information governance policy. Yet often there are basic issues that are not covered or even considered. Despite their best efforts, these oversights can be devastating to the company's operation. For example, how many large corporations have any sort of policy—or for that matter have discussed with their employees—governing the use of USB drives for saving and transferring data? What is on that thumb drive that you picked up at the last trade show? Could there be malware purposefully planted on the device? Did your home computer transfer a virus to the thumb drive that you are now bringing to work? As minor as the issue of a thumb drive may seem to be, the potential consequences to the company's computer system are significant.

One executive of a 5,000-person company (who wished to remain anonymous) reported to us that everyone in the organization has extensive safeguards in place and receives annual refresher training on information governance security. For example, this company has a policy that prohibits employees from e-mailing documents from their work to home computers, or vice versa. For transporting documents, employees are issued a specific work thumb drive, which is scanned for viruses after being brought back into the office before any files can be copied to an office computer.

## LEGAL ISSUES AND E-DISCOVERY

Large companies often find themselves on the receiving end of litigation. Litigation means discovery, and discovery means turning over records to opposing counsel. A good information governance policy not only serves to protect the company, but actually eases facilitation of things such as legal and electronic discovery (e-discovery). In case you are wondering about e-discovery, it is simply the legal process where electronic records relevant to a legal matter are discoverable. It can be a massive undertaking in today's world of big data.

An information governance policy does not just prepare you for an e-discovery request. It also ensures you have only the information necessary for the request. A large part of any information governance policy is a retention policy. It is not just securing and maintaining the data you have; it is knowing when and what to delete. Because policies are in place covering how information is retained and stored, retrieval is streamlined. This enables a large company to comply with court instructions without unnecessary or costly time and effort.

The anonymous company executive mentioned above further reported that information governance does not hinder their business operation, but instead "helps us do business lawfully and ethically while protecting our information assets."

Likewise, when we surveyed Ahmed Mahrous of the Hilton Corporation, he reported that his company's information governance policy prevents the unauthorized release of sensitive information. Based on established Hilton policies, Mr. Mahrous indicated that "all guest information is maintained as strictly confidential and secured in our systems, and only released by specific legal requests or proper law enforcement channels."

## REGULATORY COMPLIANCE ISSUES

Various government entities, such as the Food and Drug Administration and Department of Agriculture, are responsible for regulating how companies conduct their business, and these entities focus specifically on large public entities. Ensuring compliance for your specific industry is an obvious management responsibility, and most large companies are well aware of such regulations and structured to ensure compliance. Information governance helps to ensure compliance for those that need to work within the boundaries of industry and governmental regulation while managing stakeholder expectations.

Additionally, corporate responsibility acts such as Sarbanes–Oxley drive leadership to take a proactive stance on protecting the company. Corporate governance in general and information governance in particular encompass the actions necessary to protect the enterprise and provide some protection for those with oversight *if* something were to occur. When you think of the damage done to a company during a major breach of clients' personally identifiable information, you think of the loss of reputation, the loss of revenue, and the loss of market share. Without an information governance plan, the loss can also be felt personally and financially by those who are responsible for managing and overseeing the company.

## HUMAN RESOURCES

Human resource departments at companies of all sizes are driven by information. The records kept and the policies in place can be the difference in how well your people are managed and how effective your defense is in relation to legal action regarding employee issues. A truly forward thinking information governance policy will head off problems before they start by requiring a thorough vetting policy in the hiring process. Remember that architectural firm where the employee left with all the design work and clients? The problem might have been avoided if only they had implemented a system to weed out problem employees or—at the very least—a system to track and hold people accountable.

Likewise, a well-communicated information governance program will instill confidence in employees. They will understand what they can and cannot do, and they will have a clear understanding of threats and benefits to properly managing employee data as well as that of their customers. The direction information governance gives to employees is an important part of a satisfied and focused work group. It leaves little ambiguity.

## THREATS UNIQUE TO LARGE BUSINESSES

A large business can face a whole host of threats that a smaller company might never encounter. Whether it is large-scale computer intrusion to the company's servers or the individual executive who is targeted by a spear phishing attack, a comprehensive information governance plan can prevent damage from occurring. Our chapter on large businesses spells out threats large entities face, including the threat of a small-scale attack that the attacker hopes will go completely unnoticed.

### BUSINESS MANAGEMENT PRACTICES

Lisa Daniels, Managing Partner of KPMG's Arizona Practice/Risk Consulting, answered a few questions for us and described how information governance is integrated in her large company. "KPMG has a very robust information security and confidentiality compliance program that includes policies and procedures, training and monitoring through various functions within the organization. The policies were developed through our compliance office with input from various key areas of the business and then approved by the Board. It assists in achieving our goals given the highly confidential information we deal with each day." You don't have to be a company like KPMG to benefit from such practices, but if you are a large corporation, information governance is crucial to ensuring the success of your operation.

## What You will Learn

### OUR BUSINESS FIRST FOCUS

In the subsequent chapters, we will show you that information governance is designed to protect your business without getting in the way of your doing business. In fact, you will learn how to manage your company better and think differently about the information you possess or are developing. Every policy and procedure has been designed for smooth implementation without disrupting the flow of your company's operation. Information governance is a basic management responsibility, and while every company has unique issues and problems, some fundamentals of information governance should be adopted by all.

### MANAGEMENT, NOT IT: A NEW WAY OF THINKING

Until now, all information governance efforts were thought to be the responsibility of the IT professional in your office. Information governance needs have grown steadily in recent years, however, and many of the issues are now outside of the framework of traditional IT boundaries. Information governance has to be the concern of everyone in the organization, and leading the efforts can no longer be relegated to one small group of individuals who possess technical expertise but have little influence over different divisions within the company. Management must set the example from the top down and lead the way. In the twenty-first century, information governance will be a concern of all aspects of business and must be addressed by senior leaders of the organization. Adopting a whole-company approach to cyber security and prevention of data breaches can help companies mitigate the negative impact of cyber incidents.[5]

Connie Robinson, who for years has been on the executive committee of a global nonprofit organization, shared with us an example of how her colleagues did just this by taking the lead in developing information governance plans. "The governance policy was developed by the governance and HR executive committees. The chair of the governance committee oversees the implementation of the policies. It definitely assists in achieving goals. As goals are established, the governance helps the board to understand and be focused for ensuring consistency."

This top-down approach is appropriate, as it sets the stage for the rest of the organization. Information governance is no longer a "nice thing to do" or something that has no name and is handled by the senior IT people, an IT contractor, or the HR department. It is a management function that must be understood, developed, and managed by the most senior members of the management team. The attention paid to information governance will pay dividends to any organization that has the fore-sight to develop the policies, procedures, and—most importantly— culture that are information governance.

In subsequent chapters, we will tell you what a good information governance policy is for different sized organizations. We'll also explain the threats that exist in today's world and how your policy will help to defend against them. This, in turn, will increase your marketability and your company's performance by improving efficiency and effectiveness. Finally, and perhaps most importantly, in the concluding chapters we will help you to develop a policy that is appropriate to your organization and will be part of the day-to-day operations for your company.

# References

1. Ponemon Institute, *Managing Cyber Security as a Business Risk: Cyber Insurance in the Digital Age*, August 22, 2013.
2. Ibid.
3. Russ Johnson, Personal Communication, October 4, 2013.
4. Matthew Fehling, Personal Communication, October 13, 2013.
5. Ibid.

# Chapter 2

# The Threats of Today and Tomorrow

As long as there have been computers, there have been issues concerning computer security. Even before computers became mainstream, hackers broke into telephone computer systems to obtain free long-distance service. (Apple founders Steve Wozniak and Steve Jobs were rumored to be "phone phreaks" back in the day.) It is no surprise that with the advent of computers into our everyday lives, corresponding security issues would arise to threaten the safety and security of our important information.

Today we all have smart phones on our hips, tablets in our hands, and other devices generating enormous amounts of data that we need. Can you imagine intentionally leaving home without your smart phone or iPad? All our information—banking, e-mail, and other proprietary data, as well as the history that accompanies each keystroke transaction—is registered somewhere. It is a scary cyberworld out there, and it is becoming more frightening as technology moves forward.

Today's criminal element possesses a high degree of technical skill. The number of these criminals continues to grow, as does their technical abilities. Think of it this way: criminals over the age of forty-five did not grow up around computers the way today's children are doing. The kids and young adults of today are tech savvy. It is natural for them because it has been such a large part of their lives. They don't know a world without personal computers, smart phones, and the Internet. To them, this is how the world has always been. Technology is second nature, and it will continue to be second nature for their kids and future generations.

As these tech-savvy generations grow older, the percentage of technically proficient individuals will increase exponentially. As that happens, some will choose crime as a means of making money, and these individuals will turn to the means with which they are most familiar—technology. What that means for cyber security is that over time the volume of threats will increase as more and more of the criminal element gravitates to the ease of technology. As technology continues to advance, the sophistication of the crimes will increase as well.

A further complication to this problem is that business owners of today and tomorrow purposefully seek out employees that have the technical skill-sets to advance their companies' agendas. In doing so, there will inevitably be the occasional hire of a misguided individual who uses these skill-sets to damage, steal, or destroy their company's important information.

This new world of advancing technology and technical skills means we need to look at things differently. We must learn from the mistakes of others. But considering the astonishing rate at which technology is advancing, keeping pace with the changing landscape of threats can at times seem overwhelming. A well-conceived and implemented information governance plan can make the difference between success and failure. The challenges posed by changing technology and the accompanying threats cannot be ignored. As stated at the end of chapter one, it is not a matter of whether you will become a victim, but rather when.

## Defining Threats

Understanding the various threats is essential to properly defending against them. The threats in the cyberworld are not limited to a nefarious person sitting in front of a computer monitor in some far off country. Of course, those persons are in fact out there and do commit those types of attacks every single day. Sadly though, the threats businesses encounter today are far more numerous and often closer to home.

In a survey of business professionals conducted by the authors, the general consensus among the respondents was deep concern about confidential information becoming compromised by the acts of a third party. Our respondents further expressed concern regarding the damage to the reputation of their companies as a result of such an attack and the financial impact that would most certainly follow. "Help us protect our data" was the consistent refrain. Additionally, as much as business owners worry about their reputations and their money, the underlying concern was how all of this might impact future business opportunities.

As determined by the Ponemon Institute, the below chart[1] represents a breakdown of the most common impacts resulting from data breaches during a recent twenty-four month period.

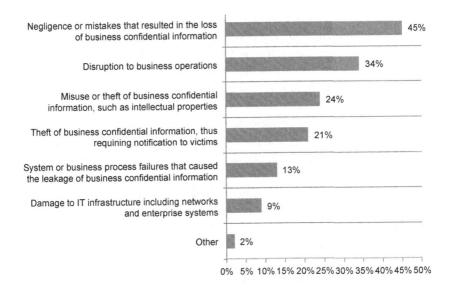

Let's take a look at the different means that can be used to perpetrate a scam, commit a crime, or cause a disruption to your business. What follows is a list of areas that need to be considered when developing an information governance policy comprehensive enough to offer protection while not so restrictive that it prevents you from accomplishing your business objectives. This balance between business operations and security is important whenever developing an information governance plan. You do not want to wreck your business while trying to protect your business.

## Hardware

You probably know that hardware in the computer world is exactly what it sounds like. It is the physical equipment used to produce, transmit, and store electronic information. Hardware is the computer, the monitor, the server, the switch, the fax, the printer, the scanner, and every other piece of equipment that gets plugged in, synched, connected wirelessly, or made interactive with your computers in some way to carry out electronic tasks. This is your network. It is the circulatory system for your business. Just as blood moves through your body to keep it alive, data run through your network to bring the components needed to operate a healthy business. With a system that is configured correctly and managed appropriately, your network stays healthy.

Stop for a minute and think about where most—if not all—of your electronic equipment is manufactured. Numerous foreign countries are producing computers, chips, routers, and most other hardware for users in the United States. China is one of the largest exporters. The labor may be inexpensive and the technology sound, but at the same time this foreign production is creating a scenario were US-based companies are exposing themselves to electronic espionage. Because there is no oversight on this foreign production, the possibility exists that chips and other components manufactured for computers bound for the United States might have malware pre-installed, enabling others to see your information or—even worse—destroy the information at will. The scenario becomes even more of a concern when you consider the number of private companies in the United States that work as defense contractors. Think about all the proprietary business information that can be stolen, much of which relates directly to our own national security. Likewise, think about the loss of money invested to produce these products and technology, as stolen proprietary information is being used by foreign competition.

Although such a scenario may sound far-fetched, those in the IT world—particularly those fighting the ongoing cyber war—understand this is a real occurrence that is happening every day. We are under attack, but most people do not even realize it is occurring.

A recent example is a company located in the Southwest that purchased servers manufactured overseas. The servers were checked several times and scanned prior to installation on the network. After six months of stellar performance, the company noticed a spike in out-going information which was caused by pre-installed malware. Fortunately, the information sent was not a national security issues, but it could have been had the company been a defense contractor.

The development of a network or the purchase of a single laptop are decisions that need to be made carefully and with your information's security in mind. Equipment manufactured in other countries can add a level of threat to which you may not wish to be exposed. Although few options other than foreign businesses are available when purchasing computer equipment, the means do exist to mitigate such a threat and protect your data. Being aware and designing your company around good procedures are the first steps. Be proactive, stay alert, and be aware of the changing landscape. Utilize trained persons that understand the threat matrix of today and know how to analyze and evaluate potential issues arising from these equipment purchases.

## SOFTWARE

When you think of software, you probably think about common programs such as Microsoft Office, Adobe Acrobat, and other applications designed to perform specific tasks such as word processing or accounting. But software is a lot more than just what you see and use on the computer screen. Every computer, server, or portable device has an underlying operating system that directs how the device works. These systems are only as good as the software that is installed on the device. Software can pose a threat to your information's security in the form of malicious software. Such programs—commonly known as malware—will be addressed later in this chapter.

The best way to protect against nefarious software is to use an original off-the-shelf product taken straight from the box. Just as you are cautious in your purchase of hardware, the same level of concern must also be taken when obtaining software. Be cautious as to where and from whom you obtain any software that you plan on using on your computer system.

Some people have tried to save money by utilizing pirated software. Pirated software is a program that has been illegally copied. It is often resold either as a purported original product or a used product at a reduced cost. Obviously, this is illegal, and the software industry has implemented programs that offer rewards for turning in companies that use pirated software. Aside from the obvious ethical considerations, the use of pirated software will generally prevent you from obtaining program updates offered by the manufacturer. These updates contain not only fixes and improvements to the software program but also patches that prevent the unauthorized compromise of your computer program (and computer) by unknown persons.

Another significant concern is that pirated software may have been altered or be infected. Installation of such programs can cause serious computer damage. If you rely on others to provide your software, make certain they are not cutting corners. You should have a system in place to verify that you are only using legitimate and legal software. Keep your software and licensing agreements current in order to have the latest version with the most recent technical fixes and protections. A good information governance policy will cover all of this by having in place regular reminders to do so.

## MOBILE DEVICES

More and more, people rely on mobile devices to carry out everyday functions. With the increased reliance on today's mobile devices, criminals have developed software specifically designed to threaten and compromise these important devices.

Different types of devices use different operating platforms. As operating systems like iOS and Android become more commonplace in the mobile device world, so will be the viruses specifically created to attack these platforms. A virus specifically designed to attack a cell phone can be spread to other cell phones via the cellular network on which they operate.

Of the many applications a virus can have on a mobile device, one example is bluejacking, which is a means of sending unsolicited messages to a third party from the victim's mobile device. By using Bluetooth technology, a criminal can remotely access the victim's cell phone. These messages might include pornographic images or threatening messages. Because bluejacking makes it appear as if the victim is sending the message, it obviously can be damaging to both the business and the reputation of the mobile device owner.[2]

A threat similar to bluejacking is bluesnarfing. Bluesnarfing also makes use of Bluetooth technology, but instead of sending information it allows criminals to retrieve data from wireless devices such as cell phones and laptops. Considering the information you keep on all sorts of devices, this type of data theft can obviously include your contacts lists, written data, and images. The images stolen can include not only personal photos but also schematic drawings and other proprietary information.[3]

Have you seen the acronym BYOD? It stands for "bring your own device." Many companies are moving to a model where employees are allowed to use their own personal devices—such as tablets and smart phones—for all work-related activities. This is a great idea for the company as a means of cost savings. It can also attract employees that are comfortable and effective with already familiar devices. Keep in mind, however, that managing such a corporate policy can present difficulties for your business security.

When a company issues a device to its employees, the company can dictate the means and methods by which the devices can be used. But when a private party legally owns the device, the company has no authority over its operation. The device may not use encryption, and worse yet the operating systems may not be up-to-date. All of this makes the device vulnerable to potential attacks—including bluejacking and bluesnarfing—while hosting your company's important information. The user might not even have a passcode lock in place which means the information can be accessed by anyone who has possession of the device. From a security standpoint it might be less expensive, in the long run to supply your employees with the portable tools they need to do their jobs.

## VIRUSES

A computer virus is a piece of computer code designed to have a negative effect on a computer. This negative effect can range from corrupting portions of the system to destroying all of the data contained within. Unfortunately, new viruses are being developed every day, which can make it challenging to stay in front of the threats. Fortunately, there are many powerful tools on the market that can help minimize your risk.

The antivirus programs on the market vary a great deal. Some are designed to work on single machines while others are designed for enterprise-wide distribution. As in the case of all software used by your business, you need to be sure that you are using a product that has the right level of protection to meet your specific needs. The application of this particular information governance security policy cannot be the job of just the IT department. Rather, the policy must be understood by all employees and be made part of a company-wide system that is followed at all levels.

No antivirus program is 100 percent effective. Vigilance and systemic processes to conduct regular checks to ensure no virus has infected your company's computer system are essential for business safety and security.

## MALWARE

Malware is a malicious piece of computer code or application that can damage your computer, your network, and your data. Malware is the means by which a computer is infected by a virus. Malware is software designed for the sole purpose of transmitting a virus to a computer system. The malware can be transmitted in a number of ways, including by e-mail with an attachment or through the user clicking on a malicious link. In such cases, the download of the malware is often the result of social engineering on the part of the person spreading the virus. Although we will address social engineering in more depth in chapter 6, the answer to protecting your business interests is ensuring that your company has written policies regulating such actions and that your employees are properly trained on a regular basis.

## CYBERCRIME

Computer crime is one of the fastest-growing types of illegal activity both in the United States and globally. While the Internet connects us and is a valuable work tool, we have also been introduced to a whole new world of criminal activity. Many things that criminals can do in the physical world can now be done in the virtual world. At present, the FBI's Internet Crime Complaint Center receives approximately 21,000 complaints per month from persons who have been the victim of a crime committed on the Internet.[4] This does not include the many others who have been victimized but do not take the time to make a report. Furthermore, many people have been attacked but are not yet aware they are victims.

So what is a cybercrime? The following sections discuss some of the most common online criminal practices that can affect you and your business.

## DENIAL OF SERVICE ATTACKS

A denial of service attack (commonly referred as a DoS attack) is an attempt by a party to make the victim's computer or computer network unavailable to legitimate users. This is accomplished by overloading the victim's computer network with too much information. One such method is by continually sending the system thousands of e-mails simultaneously. The attacker can accomplish this by remotely using multiple computers that have been illegally taken over and programmed to carry out this task.

The easiest way to understand a DoS attack is to imagine yourself standing on a stage in front of an audience. Someone asks you a question, and because only one person is talking, it is easy for you to hear and respond to the query. Now picture yourself standing on a stage with several people in the audience shouting out questions at the same time. You might be able to make out the different questions, but it is more difficult to process your answers and respond to each person in a timely manner. Now picture being on stage with the entire audience is shouting questions at you simultaneously. Nothing makes sense, and your brain goes on overload, causing you to be unable to respond at all. This is what a DoS attack is like to your computer.

Major retail corporations have experienced DoS attacks. They are done for a variety of reasons, including vandalism or an attempt by a competitor to inhibit sales. Political websites have also experienced DoS attacks, sometimes to make a candidate look as if his or her website is unprofessional and other times to make a political statement.

In some cases, the victim will be contacted by the attacker, who will agree to discontinue the attack if the victim pays a fee. This illegal practice is known as ransomware. Your information governance policy should have plans to deal with these types of situations, including contact information for any law enforcement departments you would need to contact to have action taken immediately.

## HACKING

In the computer security world, a hacker is someone who seeks to exploit weaknesses in a computer system or network. Hackers can be motivated by profit, a desire to protest, or even just the challenge of taking on some entity that is powerful, such as your business or the government. Generally, such persons who purposely attempt to penetrate computer security for malicious purposes are known as black hat hackers (as in the bad guy wears a black hat).

Within the hacking community, hackers often share their secrets and techniques with others. Not all hackers are out there hacking for nefarious purposes, however. In the hacking world, a person known as white hat hacker attempts to break computer security for non-malicious reasons. They are often hired to test the security of a company's computer system and look for weaknesses that you should fix. Employing a white hat hacker might be a wise measure to ensure your system is properly protected.

## SPYWARE

Spyware is software that enables a user to obtain information covertly off another person's computer or other electronic device. Spyware can be placed on the victim's computer in the same way a virus can; through the use of malware. The purpose of spyware is to allow the user to view the victim's computer and all of its important information without the victim ever knowing about it.

## SOCIAL ENGINEERING

In the world of information security, social engineering refers to the practice of psychologically manipulating people into divulging confidential information or performing actions that they would otherwise not do. As human beings, we are genetically wired to try to be helpful, which is how criminals capitalize on social engineering.

Those engaging in social engineering often use a pretext, creating some type of exigent circumstance so that the victim feels it is imperative that they assist. This sort of pretext could include a call from an individual who claims to be with your company's IT department who needs your password to resolve a problem within the company's computer system.

Another example of social engineering is known as *quid pro quo*, i.e., you give me something and I will give you something in return. Again, an attacker may call a company employee claiming to be offering technical support for the victim's existing computer problem. In making random calls to various company numbers, it is only a matter of time before the criminal eventually stumbles across an employee who is having some sort of computer problem or issue. The attacker will offer to "solve" the problem by having the victim cooperate with the caller's instructions. The caller may ask for the employee's password or other identifying information directly or may steer the victim to a web link that will download malware onto the computer system.

Not too long ago, the authors decided to test their own social engineering skills in order to demonstrate how easily it can be done. While speaking at a business conference, the authors told the audience that they were having a contest to determine the audience's skill level in coming up with secure passwords. The audience was invited to write their passwords on the back of their business cards and pass them forward to the stage. After first providing assurances that the passwords would be shared with no one else and destroyed afterwards, the authors explained they would review the passwords to determine which was the strongest, and the winner would receive a prize. Despite the fact that we were in a session on keeping your personal information secure, it is not surprising that almost everyone chose to play and willingly provided this sensitive information.

## PHISHING

Phishing is a technique criminals use to fraudulently obtain private information. In most cases of phishing, the criminal (known as the phisher) will send an e-mail that appears to come from a legitimate source, such as your bank or credit card company. The e-mail will request a verification of your personal information, such as your social security number, date of birth, bank account number, or PIN. Because all of this information has been given to the financial institution on previous occasions, most people give little thought to what appears to be a legitimate request. Additional pressure to provide the information usually involves some sort of warning or threat that the victim's account will be suspended if the requested information is not provided. Under such circumstances, many people are all too eager to comply with the request.

Generally, these e-mails will have a link that will purportedly take the victim to the bank's website where they can update their account information. Of course, this link is a way for the criminal to obtain the victim's personal information for fraudulent use. Once again, regular training to educate and remind employees of these threats is the key to keeping your business secure.

## SPEAR PHISHING

Spear phishing is a specific type of attack that focuses on a particular individual. Most prominent persons within an organization will have their names and bios on the company web page. Many others will have their professional resume on job sites like Monster.com And many have their professional histories listed on LinkedIn. The spear phisher need only review any of these sites to obtain specific data on a particular individual. By knowing details of the victim's professional life, the criminal—whether contacting via phone or e-mail—has greater credibility and may seem legitimate, which puts the victim at ease. Often, the spear phisher will claim to be calling from the victim's own human resources department in order to update their files. Under this type of scam, the victim can not only give up personal information that will hurt them but may also give up proprietary information that will harm the company.

## BAITING

Baiting is a method that takes advantage of our natural curiosity. It is used by criminals to place a virus on your computer. Say, for example, you were to find a thumb drive on the floor or out in the parking lot of your company. Let's say further that the thumb drive was marked "private." Most individuals would want to run right to their desks and plug the thumb drive into their computer in order to find out what is on the device or determine its owner. In any case, the thumb drive can contain a virus designed to infect your computer with spyware or worse.

Think for a minute about the last trade show you attended. Remember all those thumb drives being given away at the vendor booths? Were any of those venders your competition? You might want to think twice before accepting and using a thumb drive given to you by an unknown person without having the device inspected for malicious software.

## TAILGATING

The world of information governance is certainly not just limited to cybersecurity. For example, tailgating is a method of compromising today's computer technology in order to conduct nefarious activities in the physical world.

Many of us wear access badges at work that record our comings and goings as we move through doors and about the office. How many times have we held the door open for others who are wearing the same badge? But is that a real badge and does that person really work for your corporation? Even if the badge is valid, its wearer may be someone who has had his or her privileges revoked. (This becomes an even more important issue in today's era of workplace violence.) It is in our nature to be kind and polite, but before holding a door open, make sure the person passing through is not using your access to gain unauthorized entry. A solid information governance policy will outline specific rules for company employees to follow so that all understand what is necessary.

## GOVERNMENTAL THREATS

What do security threats to government operations have to do with the private sector? Many businesses have the government as a client in one form or another. Private businesses can provide goods to the government or serve as governmental contractors. If you do business with the government, their information security problems then become your information security problems.

Complicating this problem is the fact that the government tends to be a very visible target. Unlike crimes where the criminal wants to make a quick getaway, information security intrusions allow the criminal to sit back and watch the results. In addition, because these types of attacks are so high profile, other like-minded criminals have the opportunity to watch the results, to learn what worked and what did not, and then to make the necessary modifications for their own future attacks. Historically, attacks against the government's information security are less about misappropriating information (although that is a common occurrence) and more about damaging or destroying data. Many government websites—from the White House on down—have had issues with damaging intrusions.

If problems with our government's computer security were not bad enough, businesses also have to be aware of threats caused by foreign governments. The theft of intellectual property by China, Russia, and other nations has been well documented over the years. It is much easier to simply take the information from someone than it is for these foreign nations to spend billions of their own dollars on research and development. When this happens, the developers here in the United States lose years of effort and billions of dollars due to the theft.

Likewise, the foreign governments engaged in these types of activities may also wish to simply destroy what has been built. For example, in the 2012 cyber attack against the Saudi Arabian national gas company Aramco, about 35,000 hard drives were wiped clean.[5] Imagine having that type of attack directed at your organization or at someone with whom you are conducting contract work.

Another big difference in these types of crimes is the level of response. If your company were the victim of a physical terrorist attack, all levels of law enforcement would get involved and do what they could to protect you. When the attack occurs in the cyberworld, law enforcement will likely view it as a cost of doing business—unless there is a significant national interest. This means the recovery efforts and future protection is left up to you.

## CYBERESPIONAGE

Just like threats from foreign governments, hackers—who may or may not be working at the behest of a foreign nation—engage in corporate espionage by targeting specific companies. According to the cybersecurity company McAfee, Chinese hackers are believed to have compromised at least five multinational oil and energy companies in "coordinated covert attacks."[6] The purposes for these attacks can range from gaining a competitive edge to targeting our national security. Not all of these attacks are committed by actual computer hacking. Corporate espionage frequently involves the use of social engineering and spear phishing.

One real-life case involved a defense contractor who was compromised by a foreign country in a very simple manner. The foreign nation accomplished their goal not through a computer hacking or a well-placed sleeper agent, but rather by placing a thumb drive in the hands of the unwitting defense employee. Several foreign nationals were able to gain entry into the employee parking lot of the defense firm where they randomly dropped a few thumb drives with the defense company logo on them. With no other identifying marks, they appeared to be company-issued thumb drives. In reality, these drives were loaded with malware that would seek out a safe place in the network to steal information and send it back to those who sought the data. All that needed to happen was for some employee to pick up a "lost" thumb drive and plug it into a computer attached to the company's network. The hidden malware would do the rest, delivering proprietary information to the attackers. In this case, although the data was at risk, the defense contractor's IT department was immediately alerted to unauthorized activity and able to mitigate the flow of information

So what happens when someone in your company finds a thumb drive with no way of identifying to whom it belongs? As mentioned earlier, we would bet that in most cases the thumb drive gets plugged into the computer of the person who found it. A good information governance policy requires such cases to be covered in employee training. It was this type of training that averted the damage to the defense contractor, as it led the employee to contact the IT department about the unusual drive. In most cases, however, employees are unfamiliar with such threats. Training and company focus can reduce such risks.

You may be thinking, "Okay, but that was a defense contractor. I don't work with the government." But remember that people look for the easy way. Criminals do not engage in these activities because they like the feeling of a hard day of breaking the law. They do so because it is easier than working for a living. Why do the work when it is easier, cheaper, and faster to steal? Do you have competitors in the United States or abroad that may think the same way? The answer is "yes, you do." Beyond a shadow of a doubt there are people that would steal from you for their own gain. Planning is the answer, and training and communication are the keys. Without it, you are exposed and vulnerable when someone comes for you and your data.

## Future Concerns

### BIG DATA

Big data is a simple way of referring to data sets whose size grows beyond the ability of software and hardware tools to manage, capture, and process in a reasonable timeframe. Big data is where the amount of data is so massive that it becomes very difficult to control. The research firm Gartner describes the challenges and upside of big data as being three dimensional: increasing volume, velocity (or speed of data transfer), and variety (or sources of data).[7]

Big data is manageable but needs oversight and thorough planning for proper utilization. Data volumes are only going to increase, and learning to manage and utilize them is what will separate well managed companies from those not effectively utilizing data. The danger in big data is that when it becomes unwieldy it becomes susceptible to compromise. Systems need to be in place to take advantage of the benefits. Those who sit idly by will be quickly passed by those with better information and access to larger amounts of information.

### DISORGANIZATION

One of the biggest threats is not being organized in the management of your business information. This is not what usually comes to mind when people think of IT threats, but it is perhaps the number one threat to your business. Without organization and structure, you are leaving yourself susceptible to the threats discussed earlier, as well as the missed opportunities for process improvement, increased productivity, and improved performance.

A lack of organization and discipline can lead to weaknesses that can be exploited. A lack of organization leads to directionless employees and lower productivity than possible. A lack of organization is sloppy and irresponsible. On the surface this is not complex. But as with many things, the devil is in the details. Your policies and procedures are the first step; managing these details is long term. If this book does nothing else, we hope it adds to your awareness and inspires you to organize your information and the processes that make information useful.

## REGULATION AND COMPLIANCE

In heavily regulated industries, the managing of data can be overwhelming. Keeping track of retention rules, document types, and formats—as well as making sure you keep only what is necessary—can be an enormous task. Add to this the sheer volume of data that is being created and you have a desperate need for organization and structure. Solid and evolving information governance will give you that structure.

Regulation and compliance does not become a threat unless the regulations are not followed and compliance is not maintained. The lack of a plan or an understanding of how to comply with different legal or governmental issues are problematic in a heavily regulated industry. A publicly held company has regulations that dictate how the company is governed and how it manages information internally and externally. The Sarbanes-Oxley Act is the most well known regulatory legislation, but other laws and regulations are also designed to protect companies, shareholders, and the public from malfeasance and mismanagement. Information security and information management are a large part of properly governing a company.

Most people think of corporate governance in terms of the finances and the future of the entity. This, of course, is true, but the management of data and information is becoming a larger part of managing any organization. The mismanagement of internal or client information can rightfully be seen as negligent.

In the legal arena, the advent of electronic discovery and computer forensics have opened doors for lawsuits, more thorough antitrust reviews, and requests for larger and better-defined scopes of information. When a merger takes place between two large companies, governmental requests for information prior to approval can be enormous. Imagine a request for all marketing, sales, and analytics in e-mails, presentations, plans, data, and information from both companies. It is not unheard of for businesses to provide hundreds of terabytes of data for legal review. The cost of the review alone can be staggering, not to mention the cost of collection, collating, and cataloging. Without a plan in place, this type of request can be devastating to the deal if not to the company itself. It is not about more; it is about better.

Futurists have discussed what is known as "Moore's Law" for years.[8] Basically, it is the conjecture that the speed of processing, memory capacity, or other technical rates doubles every eighteen months. Although this has been proven to be generally true the volume of data being produced may be happening even faster than has been produced in the past.

The amount of information, devices, nodes or points of entry, users, and the speed at which the technical world changes can be overwhelming. Just as fast as the increases in capacity are occurring, so are the techniques used to steal and destroy. Preparation for known and future threats takes time, thought, and action. If you sit and wait, assuming it will not happen to you, it likely will.

# References

1. Ponemon Institute, Managing Cyber Security as a Business Risk: Cyber Insurance in the Digital Age (August 22, 2013), p. 5.
2. "Cyber Security: Software Threats," accessed October 19, 2013. http://mediasmarts.ca/cyber-security/cyber-security-software-threats/.
3. "Cyber Security: Software Threats."
4. http://www.ic3.gov/media/annualreport/2013_ic3report.pdf, page 3.
5. John Leyden, "Hack on Saudi Aramco Hit 30,000 Workstations, Oil Firm Admits," *The Register*, August 29, 2012, accessed October 20, 2013. http://www.theregister.co.uk/2012/08/29/saudi_aramco_malware_attack_analysis/.
6. Kukil Bora, "McAfee Exposes Biggest-Ever Series of Cyber Attacks; Is China Responsible?" *International Business Times*, August 3, 2011, accessed October 21, 2013. http://www.ibtimes.com/mcafee-exposes-biggest-ever-series-cyber-attacks-china-responsible-821643/. November 8, 2013.
7. http:// www.gartner.com/.
8. http://www.intel.com/.

# The Ever Changing
# Technical
# Landscape

# Chapter 3

At the February 2014 RSA conference in San Francisco, FBI Director James Comey stated, "Given the scope of the cyber threat, agencies across the federal government—including DHS, the Secret Service, and the Department of Defense—are making cyber security a top priority. Within the FBI, we are targeting high-level intrusions—the biggest and most dangerous botnets, state-sponsored hackers, and global cyber syndicates."[1]

In May 2012, former FBI Director Robert Mueller held a similar view, stating, "Terrorism does remain the FBI's top priority, but in the not too distant future we anticipate that the cyber threat will pose the greatest threat to our country." He then added that "Today, terrorists have not used the Internet to launch a full-scale cyber attack, but we cannot underestimate their intent."[2]

The reality is that cybercrime poses a real and present threat that is far more dangerous than anything we have ever faced. The cyber war that is threatening the safety and security of our country is being fought with the same weapons that are also threatening the business world. As the weapons of this war continue to advance, the threats to both the country and businesses continue to grow.

## ▌ A Little History

By now we all know that the Internet has changed the way we do virtually everything. Whether we are conducting business, communicating with friends, sending information, or committing crimes, the Internet now plays a pivotal role in our day-to-day lives.

As with nearly all facets of life, the Internet has been a significant factor in how businesses of today grow and prosper. During the past five years, the Internet has accounted for 21 percent of the GDP throughout the world.[3] Think about the evolution of the Internet and, with it, the transference of information. Society's Internet users have evolved from a minority of persons seeking social interaction to half of the world's population performing all sorts of online functions. Of course, businesses both large and small have a significant interest in this online activity. For everything from contacting clients to conducting transactions, the Internet is essential to most business operations.[4] While large enterprises and national economies have reaped major benefits from this technological revolution, individual consumers and small upstart entrepreneurs have been some of the greatest beneficiaries of the Internet's empowering influence.[5]

Despite everything that has already been accomplished, the future remains wide open to advances in technology. These advances will be accompanied by other opportunities for the compromise of sensitive information. For example, only recently has the term *bitcoin* come into common use. It is widely used on the Internet to engage in all sorts of financial transactions, but this new form of currency raises a number of problems. Who is controlling the value of bitcoins? Who is insuring the funds? If your investments are electronically absconded, who has the proper jurisdiction not only to investigate but also convict and punish the thieves?

The impact bitcoin may have on the way we transact business is enormous. This new peer-to-peer currency is already prevalent in the online world and is growing in popularity. Imagine the security issues if it becomes mainstream. They can be frightening. Bitcoin exists without centralized control or system of regulation.

Like the security of your company's personal information, advances in technology have now introduced the problems of securing your company's finances as well. While business and government alike may welcome the opportunities the Internet provides, there must be a continued recognition of the security threats that come with these new opportunities.[6]

## ▌ The Issues

### HARDWARE/NETWORK CHANGES

Just as the Internet has evolved, so has the way we use computer hardware. Photos of the early days of computing show a single computer filling an entire room. The computing capacity of those original systems was less powerful than what we now carry on our smart phones and tablets or—in some cases—wear on our wrists.

As with computers, networks have also changed. Today's networks are much more complex and continue to evolve. Data storage is one of the largest areas of growth, which makes the proper protection in the form of data security a high priority.

According to International Data Corporation, in 2020 there will be approximately 1.9 billion computers, 2.6 billion smart phones, 2 billion consumer electronics, and 25 billion embedded and intelligent systems.[7] Because of the growth potential for computer devices and their networks, information governance policies need to adapt and consider all the issues to ensure data are secured in the most reasonable manner possible. Likewise, a multitude of other technological devices developed in the future will integrate with these computers and networks. Equal care must be given to managing those information connections.

In one extreme example of a breach of network security, one of Iran's nuclear power plants suffered a malware attack in 2012. As politicians continue to debate the level of nuclear activity Iran should have in today's world, those committing the attack raised threats that parties on all sides of the issue fear. This malware attack was able to penetrate the network's security and shut down the nuclear plant's operations. Although the attack was contained and the plant was brought back online, what if the attackers had more nefarious intentions? Rather than shutting the plant down, what if the attackers discontinued the cooling process, allowing the reactors to reach dangerous temperatures that resulted in a meltdown that released radioactive material?

Although the example of Iran's nuclear plant is an extreme one, it is a good metaphor for your own company. Are you capable of stopping an intruder from releasing information from your network? Whether they are part of critical pieces of national infrastructure or a business, networks must be protected from cyberattacks. Understanding that these attacks will happen, contingency plans must be incorporated into a solid information governance plan to ensure that important information is properly backed up and secured, so that operations can continue until the threat has been resolved.

## WHAT THE HECK IS A NETWORK?

Many people do not understand what a network actually is and does. In just a few sentences, let's describe what a network is really all about. In simple terms, a network is what allows computers to work together. A network can be immensely complex, but at the base level it is all about getting components to work together and utilize software for tasks that need to be completed. Working together nearly always includes interaction with data or with other networks and computers on the Internet. This allows diverse systems and software to work together, increasing processing and storage power by combining systems. Benefits of a network can include sharing files, securing internal communications, collaboratively sharing resources, and managing databases that store the information generated and needed by the enterprise.

Some of the terms associated with network include switch, router, server, firewall, mainframe, Ethernet, hubs, and bridges. There are even virtual servers and environments that run inside a network. There are many more possible components, but for our purposes we don't need to list them all. Suffice it to say that networks take a specialized skill-set to build and maintain.

While you do not have to know how to construct a network to have an information governance policy, you should have an understanding of what capabilities you expect your network to have. If you don't have a comfortable level of knowledge about the complexities of networks, it is a good idea from a security standpoint to have more than one person—from within and from outside your organization—take a look at your network's operation. Remember, those that manage your network or your data hold the keys to the kingdom. Chose carefully, as these highly skilled and very valuable people can be your business's best friend—or worst enemy.

## Networks that are Used for Other than Intended Purposes

One threat from the IT world that is often overlooked is the misuse of a computer network. Regulating how a network is being used—and not just who is using it—is a necessary part of an information governance policy.

Let's return to the example of bitcoin. Aside from uncovering bitcoins, which brings its own reward, miners of bitcoins have another incentive—namely, the fees they can collect for transactions by users. They are therefore motivated to include transactions in their block. This becomes a more important factor as the difficulty in creating new bitcoins increases. Many people are excited by opportunities presented by bitcoins, but technology that is slated for use in a business can be diverted to other tasks. For example, a university IT director in New York built a powerful network for the school, but during down time he was using it to mine for bitcoins. (Please see http://www.isaca.org/Certification/CGEIT-Certified-in-the-Governance-of-Enterprise-IT/Prepare-for-the-Exam-OLD/Study-Materials/Documents/Developing-a-Successful-Governance-Strategy.pdf). This stretched the capabilities of the system and increased the security risk. Another issue for the leaders at the university was whether the millions of dollars spent on the network were all essential for university operations.

Beyond the technical issues lie the more nefarious criminal elements. Your company's information governance policy should have guidelines stipulating what is acceptable behavior for those operating on your company's network. These rules should include the consequences for unauthorized deviations from this policy, including the appropriate law enforcement response in cases of criminal deviations. In recent years, thousands people have been arrested for engaging in collecting and transmitting images of child pornography, which is a violation of both state and federal law. Sometimes, this criminal conduct occurs in the workplace, unbeknownst to the employer. When the authorities become aware, this criminal activity will likely result in search warrants being executed at the place of employment, along with the seizure of equipment the criminal was using—regardless of whether it is the suspect's personal equipment or that of the company.

Having an information governance policy that outlines acceptable behavior may deter those who are prone to such criminal acts from committing them through the use of the company's network. But even if it does not deter the criminal, it may mitigate the employer's civil liability by showing that the employee was clearly operating outside of the scope of their employment.

## MURPHY'S LAW

It is important to take into account the old adage that if something can go wrong, it probably will. The staggering complexity of network architecture by its very nature makes it likely that something will malfunction. Network equipment and its continual upkeep can be expensive. The manner in which the network is managed should be stipulated as a part of your information governance program. You should also have people on your team who have the proper understanding of networks and can articulate their concerns to others.

A network will have issues, a database will become corrupt, or a server will fail. Often, multiple failures occur at the same time. Employing a team that understands their role, responsibilities, and expectations is vital. Having procedures and clear lines of communication is also important. But paramount is that those in leadership positions should have an understanding of what the potential issues are and being engaged via a solid information governance policy. You can't react to a situation about which you know nothing.

Reading this book is a good start to learning the intricacies of managing your information and to understanding how it is stored, used, transferred and produced. But information governance is an ongoing challenge and one with which leaders need to stay engaged. Technology changes quickly, and having a firm grasp of the issues effecting technology and a solid plan for managing and dealing with it are steps that must be taken in order to be successful and mitigate the inherent risks. The world is changing, and we must change with it. Information governance is about managing one of the most important issues we face.

## STORAGE GROWTH

The amount of data held globally is growing exponentially. About thirty years ago (we are being generous here; it may have been slightly more than thirty years) when the authors purchased their first computers, most computers came equipped with 200 megabyte hard drives. Today, most of us are carrying cell phones that have around eighty times this amount of memory.

The growth of data is speeding up as new devices come online and processing speed increases. This growth has lead to the fact that paper copies are largely no longer required in the business world. In the medical world, it is now mandated by law that all medical records be maintained in a digital format for the ease and efficiency of sharing with others in the medical profession. The amount of data we are generating and storing is growing on a daily basis. It is expensive to maintain, but a breach causing a loss of important data would be even more expensive.

It is helpful to understand how data is measured and to equate these measurements to something familiar. Below is a breakdown of how most data amounts are measured. While it may appear to be a little overwhelming, the explanations help put these vast amounts of data into context:

Bit: a bit is the smallest unit of data that a computer uses. A bit holds the 1s and 0s that are digital information.

- 1 bit = a binary digit

  Byte: a byte is equal to 8 bits. A byte can represent 256 states of information. One byte is usually equal to one character. One hundred bytes would of information would hold an average sentence.
- 1 byte = 8 bits

  Kilobyte: a kilobyte is 1,024 bytes. One kilobyte would be approximately the size of one paragraph of text.
- 1 kilobyte = 1,024 bytes

  Megabyte: a megabyte is 1,024 kilobytes. A megabyte was once considered a large amount of data, but no longer. The old 3.5 inch floppy disks held 1.44 megabytes.
- 1 megabyte = 1,024 kilobytes

  Gigabyte: A gigabyte is 1,024 megabytes. A gigabyte is common term used to refer to disk storage. One hundred gigabytes could hold an entire library floor of academic journals.
- 1 gigabyte = 1,024 megabytes

  Terabyte: a terabyte is 1,024 gigabytes (approximately one trillion bytes). Terabytes are commonly used for the measurement of the capacity of hard drives. This is quickly becoming the most common used measurement for data storage.
- 1 terabyte = 1,024 gigabytes

  Petabyte: a petabyte is equal to 1,024 terabytes or about one million gigabytes. It is hard to conceptualize how much data a petabyte can hold. Think of filling about twenty million four-drawer filing cabinets. That would be the equivalent of a petabyte of digital information.
- 1 petabyte = 1,024 terabytes

  Exabyte: an exabyte is 1,024 petabytes (approximately one quintillion bytes or one billion gigabytes).

- 1 exabyte = 1,024 petabytes
  Zettabyte: a zettabyte is 1,024 exabytes. The equivalent of 250 billion DVD's.
- 1 zettabyte = 1,024 exabytes
  Yottabyte: a yottabyte is 1,024 zettabytes. It would take approximately eleven trillion years to download a one yottabyte file from the Internet using high-speed broadband.
- 1 yottabyte = 1,024 zettabytes
  Brontobyte: a brontobyte is 1,024 yottabytes. The only thing there is to say about a brontobyte is that it is *a lot* of data.
- 1 brontobyte = 1,024 yottabytes
  Geopbyte: a geopbyte is 1,024 brontobytes, which is too much data to even comprehend.
- 1 geopbyte = 1.024 brontobytes

It is estimated that at the end of 2012, the digital world contained approximately 2.75 zettabytes and that by 2015 we would hit 8 zettabytes.[8] Data is everywhere, and the amount is just getting bigger. Every text, tweet, update, e-mail, video, document, and picture adds to the volume. Twenty-five years ago, companies kept filing cabinets full of information, and items needed to be purged regularly. Today we keep nearly everything on hard drives, so the need to delete information is not nearly as pressing. There are, however, legal issues and costs associated with keeping too much. We like the rule that you should keep everything exactly as long as you need it and not one day longer. A good information governance policy defines record retention rules and ensures you meet any legal or regulatory requirements.

## SPEED OF PROCESSING AND TRANSFERRING DATA

Data transmission, digital transmission, or digital communication is the transfer of data from one point to another. Data transmitted may be digital messages originating from a data source, such as a computer or a keyboard. It may also be an analog signal, such as a phone call or a video signal. The speed at which data moves and is processed is growing, and—much like the amount of data being generated—it takes an understanding of how much faster things are moving to manage effectively.

Gordon Moore, one of the founders of Intel, wrote a paper in 1965 that stated that the number of transistors on circuit boards would double every two years.[9] This became known as "Moore's Law" (Figure 3.1). It has proven to apply to processing speed and memory capacity. The increase in speed is what is at the root of the digital world. It will only get faster and more precise in how it moves.

In the last forty years, we have seen the room-sized computer making millions of computations scale down to desk size then to portable and finally to miniature.

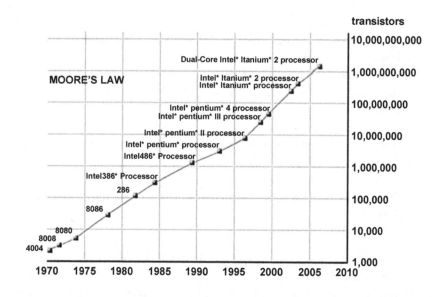

**FIGURE 3.1** Moore's Law. (http://www.ebiztutors.com/index.php/?p=313. Accessed September 12, 2013).

We carry enormous computing power in our smart phones today. What will we see tomorrow? No one knows for certain, but what is known is that without policies and procedures businesses will be left behind.

## OVERSEAS PRODUCTION

Most of the equipment being used in the United States is being built overseas. The reason for this is that the cost of production can generally be far less than what it would be if made in the United States. This overseas production, however, can raise risks to information security.

A large portion of computer equipment is being exported from China and other countries in eastern Asia. Many of these countries are home to businesses that compete with a number of American businesses. As discussed in Chapter two, it is no stretch of the imagination wonder whether malware has possibly been embedded in the machines that are being ordered from those factory and shipped to United States companies. Accordingly, your information governance plan must also take into account the inspection and malware analysis of new purchases, as well as routinely scheduled checks of existing equipment that was built overseas.

## Operating Systems, Applications, Software

Networks operate based on the software being utilized. All the advances in hardware—such as faster processors, larger storage devices, and more and faster memory—are all for naught without the software to tell them what to do.

Operating systems, the base level of computing, has had to evolve as the physical systems have changed. The operating systems of today are highly complex, dynamic systems. Software and applications are basically the same. They have grown and changed with the advent of better and faster devices upon which to run.

This has had a profound impact on how we work and live. We communicate quicker, move information faster and in greater volume, and have access to things that were impossible twenty or thirty years ago. But these great benefits do not come without problems.

Due to the complexity of these programs criminals have been able to find ways to exploit them to their benefit. New programs often have security holes in their code that are found and then exploited to gain access, disrupt operation, or steal data. These are patched as the maker of the software and antivirus companies identify them, but often these holes stay open long enough for criminals to do real damage.

A case in point is the attack on the retail chain Target in late 2013. While the investigation is ongoing, the attack was apparently the result of a malware attack that most likely occurred earlier in the year. A few things had to happen for the attack to be successful:

1. The malware had to be designed and tested before being deployed against its intended victim. It needed to run quietly in the background while sending the desired stolen info back to the perpetrators.
2. The malware had to be able to be loaded into the secure side of the merchant's network. Most often this occurs via a phishing scam or some other means of social engineering.
3. A system needed to be employed to take advantage of the stolen data.

In the Target breach, these simple steps were all taken, and the end result was some 110 million identities stolen. The depth of the problem for Target in lost revenue, loss of reputation, and possible lawsuits is still unknown. Needless to say, the dollar loss will be substantial.

Could the Target hack have been prevented? Possibly. Is it reasonable to expect entities and companies to *stop every* incident? No. The Target data breach was very sophisticated and well planned. It stemmed from another country and was very difficult to identify. Criminals are getting more sophisticated in how they attack, and all organizations—particularly large ones—need to increase their sophistication as well.

Information governance is the root of that sophistication. Having a plan, policies, procedures, and training are the first steps. Implementing those processes and making them a part of the cultural of an organization is a prudent and proactive measure that can mitigate the damage caused by existing threats.

## SOCIAL MEDIA

The first e-mail was sent in 1971. The first IRC (Internet chat) was used in 1988. Napster—a peer-to-peer file-sharing service—started in 1999. And 2003 saw the advent of many social networking and bookmarking sites. Today, Facebook, LinkedIn, Tumblr, Instagram, and other shared sites are everywhere and are a large part of many people's lives. Businesses are built on and for social networking. It has fundamentally changed the way we communicate and how we access information.

This change has arguably been for the better, but it does come with risk. The use of such sites is so prevalent that most users simply ignore or are unaware of the risks that are inherent in a system that allows people to share personal information with others so easily. Businesses that fail to utilize social networking as part their marketing and PR are at disadvantage, and those that fail to manage social networking are at a decided risk for being manipulated and taken advantage of. Employees and management need to be aware of the risks and trained to identify and address those risks.

So how do organizations get taken advantage of through social networking? Often, it happens through the release or publicizing of personal or proprietary information through a person's innocently intended use of social media. Posting job changes on Facebook or LinkedIn are well-known ways that information that should stay protected gets released. Most people are aware of this danger, but it does not take much to get caught up in the moment and type the wrong message. Once it gets published, it is out there for the world to see. Even if it gets deleted, it could have been copied and saved while it was still posted.

Information governance is responsible for making organizations at all levels better understand the issues. By establishing clear rules regarding the use of personal sites at work and clearly educating employees about why these rules are in place, risks can be mitigated. The risks cannot be removed entirely, however. They can only be minimized. People still make mistakes, and those with nefarious intent are becoming more and more savvy. Education, awareness, and constant messaging are key to this facet of information governance.

Additionally, an information governance program will clearly define levels of access. For example, a receptionist should not automatically have access to the personal information of clients and employees, because such access is not necessary to the job responsibilities of a receptionist. Keeping everyone "in their lane" is a very simple and straightforward way to minimize risks and limit exposure. Allowing everyone to access everything is dangerous and irresponsible.

## SURFING

As with social networking, web surfing can be a drain on productivity as well as increasing your risk profile. While the threat from surfing is not as prevalent as e-mail phishing scams, there are still problems with surfing. The first is the drain on productivity, which is obvious enough. Employees surfing are often just killing time. While there may be compelling reasons to surf the Internet, it is also a highly abused means of avoiding work. We believe that allowing small breaks increases creativity and improves morale. It is all about balance and keeping employees happy and driven. The risks associated with surfing the Internet stem from malware and other software that is hidden in malicious links that can cause the software to be download onto the network. There are some places from which employees should never download files. Suffice it to say a good information governance policy outlines where employees should be allowed to go and where they should not, as well as giving them a solid understanding of the risks. It is a great idea to teach people the reasons behind the rules. A little common sense and a little knowledge go a long way toward keeping employees safe while on the Internet.

## EVERYTHING IS PORTABLE

Data is portable. Such a simple statement can become a big issue if not managed properly. As the amount of storage in thumb drives, smart phones, and other devices has increased, so has the potential for large volumes of information to flow from your data storage to places you don't want to go.

In a little known case in Arizona, a mid-sized firm nearly lost all their business when a long-term employee took all customer data and all company creative information with them to a competitor when she left the company. The owners of the company had a non-disclosure agreement in place for all employees—or so they thought. This employee was never asked to complete their's as she was a "lifer." The company had no recourse. In the end, the employee did well at the new company while the company they left struggled due to the loss. A simple and thorough NDA (non-disclosure agreement), while not a 100 percent guarantee, would have made it more difficult for this to happen.

Just as flash drives provide an easy way for data you don't want on your network to be placed there, they are also an easy means for employees to steal data you don't want leaving. We have seen several security-conscious companies—and even some governmental organizations—disable the USB ports on company computers to prevent this from happening.

## MANAGING BYOD

The concept of BYOD is growing in popularity. Many company are asking or allowing employees to "bring your own device" to the job. The theory is that companies will save money through the use of employee-owned devices and that employees are more productive when they use devices with which they are already comfortable. This sounds like a great idea, right? Depending on your industry and on what tasks employees work, it may not be.

When employees bring their own devices to the work place, the control of those devices switches from the company to the employee. Even with solid controls in place, bringing a separate device to the workplace can heighten your risk. Enter into these types of agreements at your own risk and with your eyes open.

## BIG DATA

By now everyone has heard the term "big data," but we have heard some confusion regarding the meaning of the term. Simply put, it refers to instances where a dataset contains so much information that it generally cannot be managed in an existing environment.

Think about financial institutions and investment banks. These are generally considered the largest users and generators of data. The systems they have had to build in order to manage the volume of data they use are enormous. They deal with big data. So do academic research institutions and governments. As industries continue to generate more information, big data will become more prevalent and will have to be managed closely. The larger the volume, the larger the chance that nefarious activity will go undetected.

## THE CLOUD

Cloud computing is considered by many the future for the computer industry. It certainly brings many benefits, although it also raises many questions. "Cloud computing" refers to the practice of businesses utilize an interface to access programs and storage that are hosted by a cloud provider outside your company. This reduces the strain on your system, as the hard work is done somewhere else, and it allows for a reduction in cost as you grow. As an example, you would not need to buy new software for each employee; you would simply link them to your cloud solution. This reduces purchasing costs as well as possibly reducing IT staff. It sounds great, right? Now think about it differently. Your data is stored with another company and lives offsite. You access your own information via the Internet. You are not in control once it leaves your network. The cloud just went from intriguing to potentially risky.

In reality the cloud is safe for most people. In fact, we all have probably used the cloud already. Do you use Gmail, Hotmail, or Yahoo? If you do, you are using the cloud. Whether or not to utilize cloud based computing is a decision that needs to be made on a case-by-case basis. Sometimes it is very effective, but sometimes the risks and the unknowns are too great. Using the knowledge of your IT professionals and weighing the risks against the benefits should be a large part of the decision.

The cloud is here to stay and will be a part of the information technology world for the foreseeable future. Planning for it and maximizing its benefits are wise practices.

## The World is Shrinking

It is evident from this chapter that the world is shrinking. The speed at which data travels, the advent of big data, and the global reach of technology all bring us closer together and eliminate time and distance. The benefits are great, but so are the dangers. The ability to reach markets and draw on information from far off locations has changed and continues to change the landscape in which we all work. But the risks are great too, and the more we know and the closer we manage, the better off we will be.

What's next? Certainly faster speeds and greater volumes of data. How it will impact our professional and personal lives is unknown, but it will be nothing if not interesting.

Crime today travels at the speed of technology, but so does opportunity. A solid information governance program is a catalyst for maximizing the benefits and minimizing the risks in this ever-changing world. Going about our business in an unstructured way without direction when it comes to technology is more than just poor management. It is irresponsible.

## References

1. James B. Comey, "The FBI and the Private Sector: Closing the Gap in Cyber Security" (speech delivered at the RSA Cyber Security Conference, San Francisco, California, February 26, 2014), accessed October 28, 2013. http://www.fbi.gov/news/speeches/the-fbi-and-the-private-sector-closing-the-gap-in-cyber-security/.
2. Stacy Cowley, FBI Director: Cyberthreat will eclipse terrorism, CNN MONEY, March 2, 2012, accessed November 1, 2013. http://www.money.com/2012/03/02/technology/FBI_cybersecurity/.
3. James Manyika and Charles Roxburgh, "The Great Transformer: The Impact of the Internet on Economic Growth and Prosperity," McKinsey Global Institute, October 2011, accessed October 1, 2013. http://www.mckinsey.com/insights/high_tech_telecoms_internet/the_great_transformer/.
4. Ibid.
5. Ibid.
6. Ibid.
7. "Requirements Changing Rapidly, Market Success Relies on Hardware Expertise," February 27, 2013, accessed October 20, 2013. http://www.nexcom.com/news/Detail/network-security-requirements-changing-rapidly-market-success-relies-on-hardware-expertise/.
8. Dan Vesset et al., IDC: Worldwide Big Data Technology and Services, 2012–2015 Forecast, vol. 1 (March 2012).
9. Dan Woods, "How to Create A Moore's Law For Data, Forbes, December 12, 2013, accessed December 22, 2013. http://www.forssbes.com/sites/danwoods/2013/12/12/how-to-create-a-moores-law-for-data/2/.

# Chapter 4

# The Changing Corporate Landscape

As the importance of technology and digital information has grown, so have the responsibilities of those entrusted with the data. Corporate leadership is being held accountable to stakeholders regarding data management compliance, legal issues from handling external data, and effectively and efficiently handling internal data. Clients demand it, and employees expect it. The government regulates it, and stakeholders are watching it. Data is growing, and so is the visibility of managing it properly.

In this chapter, we will delve into the legal responsibilities regarding information governance. We will look at how a good information governance program better prepares an entity to handle legal issues and how we must place managing information on the same footing as finance, labor, and legal. It is no longer good enough to manage people, inventory, production, and finance (among everything else). Managing data is vital for the success of any organization. Whether you are a one-man shop or a Fortune 500 company, managing your information is important and becoming more so.

# Today's Cyber Environment

RECENT EVENTS

At least 110 million consumers are now thought to have been affected by the late 2013 Target data breach. This single breach could affect up to one third of all US citizens and cost the company billions in revenue and a large portion of their market share (Figure 4.1).

The Target data breach highlights what many consumers think: "Companies need to take responsibility for securing my data, and if they don't I will take my business elsewhere." The breach at Target, however, is just one in a long line that continues to grow. In June 2014, P. F. Chang's announced that they had been breached, and the information of up to two million consumers had been released. Many more examples can be cited, so it behooves all businesses to prepare. Information governance does this; it prepares businesses to protect their data.

The risks of not preparing are great. Civil fines, consumer backlash, and even criminal penalties are possible. If your business is prepared and has taken the steps necessary to prevent and to react to a data breach event, you are in a much better position to defend yourself legally. If you are not paying attention to this problem—for instance, if you are not PCI compliant when you need to be—you are leaving yourself vulnerable.

The good news in that your information governance program can help guide you, and experts can assist you. While the cost of preparation is not small, a lack of preparation can be expensive.

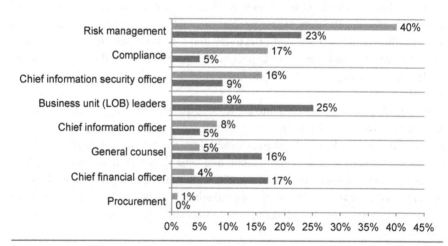

**FIGURE 4.1** Whom do companies view as being most responsible for cybersecurity risk?

The number most often associated with identity theft is $188 per record stolen. Target is the largest breach to date, and it may result in a total cost to the retailer of over $20 billion. Most businesses would not have the same level of liability even if all their records were compromised but small and midsized businesses are not often in a position to afford even a fraction of that kind of loss. Information governance can and will limit your exposure.

## LAWS AND REGULATIONS

This chapter also addresses legal issues, because a proper information governance process and policy can make organizations better prepared to handle lawsuits. Electronic discovery is commonplace in the legal system, yet most organizations are not prepared for the invasiveness and cost that can be incurred without a solid information governance plan. People, financials, and inventory are not the only parts of the discovery process these days. Data has taken a seat at the table. If you do not pay close attention, you are leaving yourself open to theft, market share loss, IP loss, and reputation degradation.

## WHERE DOES INFORMATION GOVERNANCE FIT?

Information governance is a vital piece of the management pie. As we have indicated, information governance now has a seat at the big table. There is no expectation that your information technology team will be able to solely handle all the issues and reporting that needs to take place regarding data. Truly, this management function needs oversight by the top levels of every organization.

Look at your organization today. Does it manage the data for customers and employees safely and securely? Does it remove records it no longer needs or is required to maintain, saving space and money and limiting exposure? Are the people who are trusted to handle the data and be responsible for its safety and delivery up to the task? Are they trustworthy? Are your network and all its ancillary parts managed effectively?

How do you know? The best way to know is to be actively engaged. This does not mean you have to be a computer scientist or know how to write computer code. What it does mean is that you need to have the knowledge and the interest to ask the right questions, ensure the proper procedures are in place, and verify the information given to you by those in charge of your network.

Think of it as a financial audit. In an audit, you have an outside entity look at your books. Whether your financials are compiled or audited or even if you have someone manage your daily account, you have a second set of eyes watching you finances. Information is no different. Having firm policies and procedures in place along with a verification system is vital for the growth and longevity of your company.

The laws and regulations to which you must adhere can be driven by your industry. There are laws and rules that every industry follows, and then there are the "right thing to do" items that everyone should follow. Too often, IT takes a backseat and is left open to criticism when the inevitable goes wrong. This is why an information governance policy is so important; it forces us to comply, to pay attention, and to act.

## LAW AND COMPLIANCE

Information security laws are designed to protect personally identifiable information from compromise, unauthorized disclosure, unauthorized acquisition, unauthorized access, or other situations where unauthorized persons have access or potential access to such information for unauthorized purposes. Data breach notification laws typically require covered entities to implement a breach notification policy, and include requirements for incident reporting, handling, and external breach notification.[1]

There is no one particular law that governs data breaches. Essentially, every state has different regulations and requirements pertaining to data breaches, and companies must adhere to the laws of the states in which they reside as well as those of states in which they are doing business.

Depending upon for whom the information is collected, the federal government will also have regulations that must be followed subsequent to a breach. For example, medical data would involve HIPPA. These requirements have resulted from federal privacy legislation that covers such areas as health care, securities, and in some cases the Internet. Whether state or federal, the regulations surrounding breaches seek to have information governance policies in place in order to mitigate the risks as much as possible and—when the inevitable breach occurs—to ensure anyone who might have been a victim is properly notified so that they can take steps to protect themselves.

Currently, forty-seven states, the District of Columbia, and several US territories have enacted legislation that requires notification of security breaches involving personal information. Because the companies were victims themselves, these laws do not directly hold companies accountable for the losses sustained due to the breaches. However, there remains the potential for civil litigation in the form of class action lawsuits so that the affected individuals can be compensated for their losses. While the costs of notifying thousands of victims at a time can be expensive, the prospect of having to reimburse these thousands of individuals—as we have seen in the Target breach—is frightening. Of course, lawsuits of this type generally succeed only when negligence is present. Hence, a proper information governance policy can show a good faith effort on the part of the company, which can overcome a presumption of negligence.

The nation's largest data brokers, retailers, educational institutions, government agencies, health care entities, financial institutions, and Internet businesses have disclosed numerous data breaches and computer intrusions.[2]

The Privacy Rights Clearinghouse chronicles and reports that over 345 million records containing sensitive personal information were involved in security breaches in the United States since January 2005. From February 2005 to December 2006, 100 million personal records were reportedly lost or exposed. As an example, in 2006 the personal data of 26.5 million veterans was breached when a VA employee's hard drive was stolen from his home.[3] The common denominator in these data breaches is that the attackers were seeking to obtain sensitive personal information, which they put to criminal use by means of identity theft to commit various frauds, such as taking out a mortgage in someone else's name or having credit cards issued on the victim's bank account.

If any positive has come out of the multitude of data breaches, it is that the public has become much more aware of the dangers. Just a few short years ago, most would not have given a second thought to the release of his or her own personal identifying information to a doctor's office or a business. Now, however, when asked for such information, many people will immediately wonder who will have access to this information and whether they have anything to fear regarding its security. In today's changing corporate landscape, businesses have to consider these concerns and put their clients' minds at ease, reassuring the public that they are competent at managing personally identifiable information. Failure to do so will inevitably result in the loss of the public's trust—as well as the public's business. With the variety of remedies that are available to consumers through the legal system, a breach means corporations can expect greater financial problems than just the loss of future business.

The medical profession in particular has undergone dramatic changes in the way it collects patient information and the regulations under which it must operate. By 2017, all medical records within the United States are expected to have been transformed from handwritten patient charts to online medical records. The benefits of this are obvious. Doctors with multiple offices can pull up patient records wherever they are working. Medical reports prepared by one doctor can be sent immediately to a treating specialist. If you are the victim of a serious accident or injury while away from home, your primary care physician can send all of you medical information immediately to the emergency room that is treating you. But when it comes to data breaches, this new advance in the way the medical profession retains its patient records brings with it additional dangers that had not previously existed.

Say, for example, that your medical records have been compromised, but you are unaware of it. Someone decides they are then going to use your medical records and medical insurance to receive treatment in your name. There is obviously the potential financial loss of paying another's co-pays, along with the possibility that your insurance rates might be raised or your policy cancelled. In the case of electronic medical records, the consequences can be far greater than just financial loss. What if the person using your medical records suffers from a particular illness or ailment? They might be treated with medications that will help them, but could have an adverse effect on you should you be treated by another doctor who uses these same medications. We have now entered an environment where a data breach could cost more than money; it could costs lives.

# The Federal Government

The federal government has enacted a number of legislative regulations designed to protect sensitive personal information, all of which have accompanying financial penalties for their violation. Several of these are discussed here.

## THE PRIVACY ACT

The Privacy Act is the principal law governing the federal government's information privacy program, which governs the collection, use, and dissemination of any record about an individual maintained by federal agencies in a system of records.[4] The act defines a record as "any item, collection, or grouping of information about an individual that is maintained by an agency and contains his or her name or other personal identifiers."[5]

The Privacy Act, which pertains only to the federal government and does not have applicability to private sector records, prohibits the disclosure of any governmental records without the expressed written consent of the subject whose records may be released. The act also provides legal remedies, including allowing affected individual to bring civil suits against the government.

## THE FAIR CREDIT REPORTING ACT

The Fair Credit Reporting Act regulates credit bureaus and those who used credit reports to furnish information, all of whom have a responsibility to ensure that a consumer's information is used only for permissible purposes. When obtaining credit reports on potential employees or customers, businesses have to ensure they comply with the Fair Credit Reporting Act and that the use of such credit reports are for a legitimate business purpose, such as decisions involving credit, insurance, or employment.

## RED FLAG RULE

The Red Flag Rule is an anti-fraud regulation created by the FTC in an effort to minimize identity theft. The Red Flags Rule establishes how certain types of businesses—such as mortgage lenders, banks, and other creditor institution—must develop, implement, and administer an identity theft prevention programs. The rules provide recourse when there is a victim and the rules were not followed. The law is referred to as the Red Flag Rule because prior to or during a breach, there are "red flags" or warning signs that companies should heed. A company's program must include four basic elements: (1) identify red flags specific to a particular business, (2) have procedures in place to detect those red flags, (3) act to prevent and/or mitigate the damage from red flags, and (4) maintain a red flag program within the industry. The Red Flag Rule suggests that the best manner by which to eliminate Red Flags is by instituting information governance protocols.

## THE HEALTH INSURANCE PORTABILITY AND ACCOUNTABILITY ACT

The Health Insurance Portability and Accountability Act (HIPAA) has required that computer systems be constructed to manage health information and medical records in such a way that these records may be exchanged with other persons within the medical field in the interest of better treating patients. Of course in doing so, the federal government has required that much of your personal information now be available online, which makes it susceptible to being stolen. Unlike some of the other regulations, HIPAA actually imposes a financial penalty for those in the medical profession who fail to develop and use such an electronic system. The penalty for a violation of an administrative simplification provision is $100 per violation (i.e., $100 per medical record). Obviously, those in the medical profession who comply with HIPAA need to also account for an information governance plan to ensure they are not likewise fined for a breach of this mandated electronic system.

### Privacy under HIPAA

HIPAA also addresses the privacy of individually identifiable health information. It requires the adoption of a national privacy standard. The rule regulates protected health information that is both identifiable and transmitted or maintained by those connected with the medical profession. It also limits when an individual's information may be disclosed.

## THE HEALTH INFORMATION TECHNOLOGY ACTION

Related to HIPPA, the Health Information Technology Action (HITECH Act) requires a medical office that has used the Internet in any capacity related to a person's medical records to notify the patient when a breach has occurred. This act applies to anyone maintaining records for patients, including medical offices, hospitals, and vendors. The act allows patients to have some control in protecting themselves in the event of a breach

## NOTICE OF UNAUTHORIZED DISCLOSURE OF PROTECTED HEALTH INFORMATION

The HITECH Act requires the responsible organization to notify affected individuals when it discovers that the patient's protected health information has been—or is reasonably believed to have been breached. The requirements of the act apply to entities or individuals who work with or handle the PII included in patient records. The act further states that once a breech is discovered, the affected patient must be notified within sixty days.

### NOTICE OF UNAUTHORIZED DISCLOSURE OF PERSONAL HEALTH RECORDS

The HITECH Act also includes a breach notification requirement for personal health record vendors. Organizations that have been breached are required to notify clients whose unsecured personal health information has been—or is believed to have been—breached.

## The Private Sector

### CREDIT CARDS

The credit card industry has also issued security standards and reporting requirements for organizations that handle bankcards.[6] It requires organizations that handle bankcards to conform to security standards and follow certain leveled requirements for testing and reporting. In 2005, Card Solutions of Tucson, Arizona, was a company providing services for MasterCard. Card Solutions was hacked by persons overseas who were eventually arrested by the US Secret Service. The breach itself, however, resulted in the theft of approximately forty million credit cards, and Card Solutions was required to reimburse for losses estimated at approximately twenty billion dollars.

### E-DISCOVERY

E-discovery, short for electronic discovery, is part of the legal activity of discovery, usually in a civil or government investigation or lawsuit. With the massive growth in the volume of data that is produced and held, courts have demanded that all data be discoverable. It is also very complex. It difficult to provide the exact information requested—and nothing more or less.

In the days before the advent of ESI (electronically stored information), discovery was paper based. Most often occurring during a lawsuit or government action, a judge would receive a request or have a demand, and would order that the entity provide all documents that may be relevant to the matter at hand.

The organization that was being ordered to provide the documents would cull through its files, find the documents they thought were appropriate, and provide them to the court. At that point, the court or the opposing side would begin review of the documents provided. Often, this produced a large corpus of information. The documents were delivered in banker boxes and could—depending on the case—amount to a huge volume that had to be reviewed for relevancy. There have been times during antitrust cases that the amount of banker boxes has been delivered in semi-trucks.

Let's walk through the old process in detail in order to understand e-discovery. Once the paper records were pulled and delivered to the attorneys, the lawyers designated to review—usually junior attorneys—would sit and review one document at a time. As they read the documents, they would mark them and segregate them into piles. Some documents (classified as "responsive") needed to be handed over to the court or the other side. Others were protected by attorney/client privilege, and still others were not relevant to the case. Once the initial review was completed, a second review of the responsive paperwork was carried out by more experienced attorneys in order to ensure only truly responsive data was handed over.

After the responsive data set was complete, the divulging party would hand over the data to the receiving party for their review. The same process was then followed. A room full of attorneys would go through the documents one-by-one, looking for anything that was relevant to the case. Any documents that were relevant were added as evidence.

This process was tedious, time consuming, and extremely expensive. It was also imprecise. This system relied upon people and their judgment to find the right documents and get them to the attorneys for review. Attorneys billed by the hour, and there was no way of hastening the process without jeopardizing the case. Many cases were never brought due to this process and the expense associated with reviewing an imprecise data set manually. It was not a great way to find information, but it was all that could be done with paper information and files in different locations.

## Why Should Corporate America Care?

Beyond the obvious benefits of having an information governance policy to protect a business, are there other reasons those in charge of corporate America should embrace these concepts? The answer is a resounding "yes!"

So far, everything we have discussed in this chapter has been about laws, regulations, penalties, mitigating liability, etc. All are sound financial and legal reasons for ensuring your company has a solid information governance plan. In today's corporate world, however, those who run organizations have to take into account other factors that can affect their business.

Any worthwhile corporate executive can read a financial statement or understand the principles of law by which their business must abide. Those in executive positions generally obtained their educations at good business schools and have earned their way up the corporate ladder. Yet although they have a sound grasp of marketing, resourcing, and strategy, too many of these executives are complacent about information governance, often leaving this critical mission to those within the organization who possess the necessary expertise in the subject matter and have specialized positions within the company.[7] To these executives, this may appear to be a practical way of conducting business, but what they do not realize is that in the process they are foregoing opportunities that could enhance their company's business model.

In today's business environment, a successful company needs to strive to have transparency within the organization. Proper information governance planning and implementation, with the full support by those in charge of corporate decision-making, will set the tone for the company. Likewise, this type of forward thinking will easily make the distinction for all employees of the important role of information governance.[8]

Transparency is good for business for many reasons. Knowing that your company takes seriously the securing of sensitive information is reassuring to your customers. Through the transparency of your information governance program, the customer can understand the positive values that drive the corporation, and will better know what to expect when conducting business with your company.

When employees understand what is being done with information governance, why it is being done, and the proper way the organization's information governance program should be implemented, the employees' jobs become clearer. This transparency allows employees to become more vested in the mission and take on ownership of their role in the information governance process. Work becomes more organized and streamlined, which results in the ease of performing more functions. Simplification of work processes results in job satisfaction, and this—in turn—results in happy employees, which is never a bad thing to have in the corporate world.

Corporations can also gain a competitive advantage over their rivals through instituting information governance processes. "Good governance lowers the transactional frictions, risks, and costs associated with having unknown stakeholders with differing requirements involved in a decision."[9] Known decision-making processes enable better scoping of solutions and more effective tendering. Through these processes, companies can be better organized, causing their work to be performed better, faster, and with greater levels of success.

"General acceptance of the need for governance raises the standard for how IT solutions are framed, procured, implemented, and managed." Consequently, company projects are less likely to encounter problems that have not been anticipated. The corporation will also not incur additional costs or risk, and can avoid unnecessary potential negative publicity for either the corporation or the customer.[10]

Information governance is also good for the customers. Customers who know that their data—whether personal and proprietary—can be kept safe and secure are more inclined to be comfortable in conducting business. By outlining what the corporation's information governance policies and that the customer's information security will be assured, customers will have a clearer understanding of the company's expectations and values, which results in a deeper comfort zone in conducting business.

## MEASURING THE CORPORATE VALUE

The problem with doing anything different or innovative in the private sector is that most believe there must be an immediate financial benefit for having incurred the cost. Inherently, this is one of the issues to overcome with corporate acceptance of information governance. Information governance is not necessarily measured by what is achieved but rather by what is prevented. Hence, to receive no immediate or direct tangible benefit can actually be the sign of success.

Every dollar that is spent is a dollar out of the company coffers. There has to be an education process in place not just about how to implement information governance but also how to measure its success. Without this understanding, it may be difficult to receive continued corporate support for such policies, whether that support is managerial or financial. Therefore, those wishing to drive these policies and ensure the necessary support must also be prepared to discuss the benefits as they are measured against other less protected organizations or improvements the corporation has made over prior years without such policies having been in place.

## CLOSING CORPORATE THOUGHTS

As technology took over the workplace, so too did the need for structured compliance in order to ensure uniformity. As you can tell from the laws and regulations covered in this chapter, the need is great for a written policy on how your data and network are maintained and managed, while the benefits of having such a policy are numerous. Companies perform more efficiently, customers receive greater assurance and security, and everyone benefits from greater success.

Implementing information governance on a corporate level as technology continues to advance is a challenge all organizations today must face, and it is one that leaders of today and tomorrow must be willing to take on. If they don't, they can be sure their competitors will.

## References

1. Ponomen Institute, 2013 Cost of a Data Breach, Global Analysis, May, 2013.
2. Gina Stevens, *Federal Information Security and Data Breach Notification Laws* (Washington, DC: Congressional Research Service, 2010), 14–16.
3. Ibid.
4. Ibid., p. 2.
5. Ibid., p. 4.
6. Ibid.
7. Ibid.
8. Standards Australia, *The Value in Governance of Information Technology* (Sydney, Australia: Standards Australia, 2012), 2, p. 4, accessed on March, 2014. http://www.standards.org.au/Documents/SA-Value-in-Governance-in-IT.pdf.
9. Ibid, p. 3.
10. Ibid.
11. Ibid.

# Chapter 5

# How Information Governance Fits in the New World

Creating, implementing, and maintaining an annual business information governance policy has to be a reflection of operating in today's new world. Today's new world requires every business and organization to safeguard information from the challenges of people, technology, and regulatory requirements. In order to succeed, businesses must focus on implementing a holistic approach to educating all employees on a number of issues.

## Issues in the New World

Every employee needs to understand that the new standard in being a successful business in today's world is to be a safe and secure business. With high profile data breach events taking place each week, information security and governance is no longer just about information technology. Instead, information security and governance is about a holistic approach where every employee and every department of an organization has a responsibility to keep information safe and secure.

Employees need to stay current on how its organization manages the collection, usage, storage, and transmission of sensitive and confidential information. Additionally, employees also need to understand how prepared their organization is in detecting internal and external threats, and that the company has a data breach response plan in place to support any data breach of both current and former employee or customer information. Figure 5.1 illustrates how companies are viewing the risks to data verses other more commonly known risks—such as theft and fire—with which companies have dealt for years.

In 2012, the *Verizon Data Breach Investigations Report* identified a common theme pertaining to the loss of sensitive information; demographics. Regardless of the size of an organization, all were experiencing data breaches via being hacked. Although different industries are getting breached for different reasons and with various methods of attack, no business was safe from the threat of being compromised.[1]

A critical response to the increasing data breach trend and cyber security threat is implementing an annual employee security awareness training program where employees are required to complete an annual review of the information governance policy of the business.

For employees to be aware of security risks and vulnerabilities, it is important for them to understand two primary threats: insider threats and external threats.

## INSIDER THREATS

While most employees behave with integrity, it is always a possibility that an employee could significantly impact information security and cyber security if they simply become careless or even go rogue. This could include unsuspectingly downloading a virus or malware, stealing data, deleting business-critical files, or even sabotaging computer systems. This type of threat is often the most difficult to detect

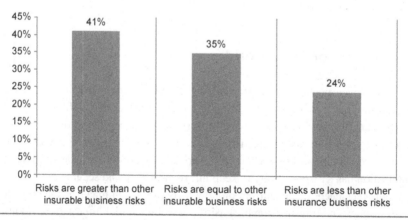

**FIGURE 5.1**   How cyber security risks compare to other risks.

since employees already have system access, and it can be challenging to distinguish normal behavior from a potential security issue.

## EXTERNAL THREATS

There is no limit to the number of outside forces that could potentially harm even the most protected IT system. These external forces include computer equipment thieves, contractors, hackers, former employees, and organized crime. Those individuals that are an external threat have a wide variety of ways to attack businesses and organizations, so employees have to be educated about some of the common techniques that are used including denial of service (DoS) attacks and phishing.

An employee security awareness training program will help your business and your employees stay informed on the most current cybersecurity and information governance practices. In due course, your employee training will become established, but employees will need regular updates and communication regarding changes in policies, standards, and best practices. Each year, every employee should complete the employee security awareness training to review existing and new information governance policies and procedures pertaining to both hardware and software.

Finally, while the completion of the employee security awareness program should be an annual action item for every employee, employees should also receive regular communications (e.g., monthly or quarterly) in e-mails and staff meetings to update them on current security trends.

## BUSINESS SIZE

A common misperception is that small or medium businesses (SMBs) do not require an employee security awareness program simply because the business is a small business with a small database. On the contrary, most SMBs—especially those with a database including personally identifiable information (PII)—are at risk of being targeted by identity thieves and hackers. The bottom line is that it only takes one event and/or device to breach any company's defenses, regardless of the organization's size.

## ROLES AND RESPONSIBILITIES

Every business needs to be clear and concise in defining the roles and responsibilities for those individuals in charge of information governance. But most businesses make a mistake by assigning the job of information security and governance to one individual. The key to a successful information governance policy is the formation of an information governance committee representing multiple employees and departments within the business or organization.

The information governance committee's responsibilities should include the following:

- Understanding the current threat environment including trends and security options;
- Creating and implementing security safeguards;
- Educate employees on cybersecurity best practices and procedures;
- Supporting cybersecurity best practices with senior management's endorsement; and
- Establishing and maintaining all security safeguards.

Management support will be critical in helping the information governance committee lead a successful and comprehensive cyber and information security objective by providing guidance ranging from document destruction to operations to policies and procedures to security projects.

Ultimately, someone needs to have responsibility. A committee is important in order to establish information governance as a cultural mainstay of the organization, but one person should have overall control. That person should not be an IT professional, although an understanding of IT is necessary. Instead, the person in charge should be more driven by compliance and adherence to policy and procedure. Many organizations utilize general counsel or the chief compliance officer, but each organization needs to make a decision that works for them. The person should be in a C-level position with this as a major responsibility. They must work closely with the IT people but be removed enough to see the broader picture.

## DATA BREACH

So what is a data breach? A data breach occurs when company information or PII is or has potentially been taken or viewed by someone who does not have the right to access the information. Saying it another way, a breach has occurred when a someone intentionally or unintentionally releases, views, or steals data. The data involved can be anything that is not in the public domain, but of particular value is PII, personal health information (PHI), company confidential information, and company proprietary information.

The most familiar type of breach is when a large company gets hacked, resulting in the loss of either customer data or corporate data. But the majority of breaches are not nearly as public. Most breaches occur due to the insider either maliciously or inadvertently taking or releasing valuable information. Also, there is the instance of an employee gaining access to areas of the company network that they should not and viewing sensitive data they should not. Often this may be a nonissue, but if this is occurring there is a good chance that other opportunities are available to those with nefarious intent.

## ACCIDENTAL VS. MALICIOUS

A data breach can be malicious or accidental. A malicious data breach event applies to a perpetrator with the objective of accessing information that could be resold on the black market or utilized to transact an identity fraud event. An accidental data breach event, while not intentional, can be just as serious depending on the type of information that has been lost or stolen. According to the 2013 Ponemon Institute data breach report, "human or system error is still the cause of almost 66 percent of data breaches."[2]

Today's regulatory environment has significantly increased industry guidelines and government compliance rules that require businesses and organizations to improve and increase their governance of sensitive or personal data to avoid data breaches. Employees need to know that data breach events are an emerging risk management issue for all businesses in all industry groups of any size. Employees also need to know that no company can prevent itself from *ever* having a data breach event. That said, businesses and organizations today are managing more customer, employee, and proprietary information than ever before.

The protection of customer, employee, and proprietary information is now a priority for all businesses and their employees in managing the risk and total cost of a potential data breach event. How employees embrace and support the effective safeguarding of information can determine the success or failure of a business when thieves attempt to steal customer and employee information, business assets, business credit information, and even the business branding and reputation for financial gain.

In recent years, identity thieves have learned that SMBs are an easier target than big companies, as big companies have more resources and have become better at protecting their assets.[3] This means that SMBs have to do a better job in educating their employees. The 2012 *Symantec National Small Business Study* found that 83 percent of SMBs do not have a cybersecurity plan in place and that developing an information governance plan should be a priority for any business.[4]

## RISK MANAGEMENT

Data breach risk management is a way to review and respond to the data breach risk factors that can negatively impact an organization. Employees need ot be aware of three primary data breach risk factors:

- People: the insider threat, whether accidental or malicious, can include current and former employees, customers, associates, vendors, and independent contractors.
- Processes: including information technology, enterprise risk management, marketing/sales, and human resources, all of which need to be aligned, defined, and documented.
- Technologies: tools on which you rely to conduct and grow your business are also being used to identify vulnerabilities and carry out cyberthreats on your business.

Data breach risk management is an important component of information governance. Such risks can be minimized by conducting pre-employment background screenings. Information technology security should be in place, including the use of firewalls and perimeter controls, anti-virus/anti-malware solutions, database security tools, and end-point security solutions. Collateral security measures should isolate and protect hardcopy employee, patient, and customer files. Vendor management should provide a review of all vendors and their security standards. Finally, an annual comprehensive security assessment can help ensure that each component is up-to-date and functioning properly.

Many organizations look at cyber risk as a non-issue, but that trend is changing. Most businesses are now putting cybersecurity on an even par with other risks. As stated earlier, the FBI takes a similar stance. Cybersecurity is important and is getting more so each and every day.

## DATA ASSESSMENT

Another important component of information governance is the completion of a data assessment of the type of information that is being collected, used, stored, and transmitted. Employee awareness of the following questions asked during data assessment will increase their understanding of and attention to information governance:

- What type of data (e.g., current and former employee records, customers information, patient information) are in your electronic and hardcopy files?
- What types of PII are included in your business data (e.g., name, address, social security number, driver's license number, bank account information, credit/debit card, medical plan information)?
- What percentage of your data involves the collection, storage, usage, and transmittal of current and former employees and customers PII.
- What aspects of your business products, services, and technology are located within and outside your business?
- What is the value of your data assets if they were stolen and made public?
- Is the data that you store subject to civil fines and penalties if breached?
- What is your overall financial risk if data you control is breached?
- In which states does your business conduct business? In what states are your current and/or former customers, employees, or patients domiciled?
- Could a data breach damage your brand? If so, what is the potential impact?
- Does your business insurance include cyber/network liability insurance?

Based on the above, every employee should be aware of their organization's strengths and weaknesses. They should know the type of questions that are asked on the self-assessment, especially the type of questions that relate to each individual employee. And—of course—they should be made aware of the result of the self-assessment.

## COST OF A BREACH

The final point on data breach risk management is the cost of a data breach. According to the 2013 *Ponemon Institute Cost of a Data Breach Report,* a data breach could cost your business up to $188 per lost or stolen record.[2] Every business or organization should therefore ask whether they have "budgeted $188 per lost or stolen record that resides in your database in the event of a data breach?"

## CHECKLIST

Creating and distributing a human resource checklist related to the information governance policy to all employees will help outline the organizational rules specific to business travel, employment agreements, internet and online access, password management, social engineering, social media, the handling of sensitive information, tablets and smartphones, portable data storage, and employee security—all of which can be gaps in information security. The human resource policy checklist is a document that states what employees may or may not do with respect to information security. It is a working document covering the rules for information security within your business. It should explain the policies and expectations to employees so that they understand the rules and the consequences for not following the policy.

Each business and organization has a unique employee skillset with unique employee experiences. This checklist is a working document that will change over time based on the employees' professional experiences and responsibilities, along with the business objectives of the organization. Below are examples that can be included on the human resource policy checklist. They should be edited to support you organizational objectives.

## BUSINESS TRAVEL

Business travel is necessary, and with travel comes the necessity to transport computers and other devices that include data and other company-sensitive information. The same threats apply to those working from home and on the road. While many airports, hotels, coffee shops, and other public places offer free Wi-Fi, free access rarely includes secure Wi-Fi. When traveling, employees need to avoid unknown and unfamiliar free Wi-Fi connections unless they are secured with a password and encryption. Caution should always be used when sending sensitive business and personal information. Employees should not send business documents and e-mails when using an unencrypted Wi-Fi connection unless a VPN is used, which will encrypt the email and its contents.

Employees should never leave their company electronics or business related documents unattended in a public location, as thefts of laptops, smartphones, and tablets are on the rise. Employees also need to guard any confidential information on their laptop, tablet, or smartphone screen from others. Anyone in close proximity—such as someone sitting in an airline seat nearby—can see what is on the screen.

Another simple, common-sense rule is for employees to make sure all their devices are password protected and are locked when not in use. Nearly all new portable devices have the ability to be locked and even encrypted when not in use. A good information governance policy will ensure that only devices meeting a set of criteria will be authorized to transact business or hold company data. Additionally, as part of the policies surrounding portable devices, the device must be locked when not in use. Many people disable this feature in order to have quicker access when they need it, but the very slight time savings is not worth the risk.

Most businesses today utilize portable storage devices (flash drives, external hard drives, etc.). These storage devices increase productivity by allowing employees to easily carry data without the need for access to a database. These storage devices need to be handled cautiously and should always be encrypted. There are USB storage devices that come with their own password protection and automatically encrypt data. But when storing data on mobile devices in the course of business, you can leave your business more vulnerable to data theft and misuse than when the data remains stationary on your network. Training and information about the risks are important, as employees will be your last line of defense. An additional item to consider is allowing employees to use their business devices for personal use. Whether it is loading applications, utilizing personal e-mail or just web surfing, employees can and will put your business in jeopardy of malware attacks, hacking, and data breaches unless properly trained and regulated.

Based on the above, every business needs to determine which types of devices to use in the business and develop a plan for the management of all mobile technology. It continues to come back to an information governance policy and training. People are your biggest threat and can be your greatest ally. When you vet them properly and give them the tools and the training, you will find more productivity and fewer threats.

## EMPLOYMENT AGREEMENT

An employment agreement is a useful tool that allows employers to communicate company policy and establish boundaries at the onset of an employment relationship. A solid employment agreement, while not infallible, creates clear expectations, explains repercussions for not meeting expectations or following procedure, and does so in a way that is easy to understand with a clear message. Information governance is a straight-forward expectation, and employees must be held accountable for following the rules.

The employment agreement should include the specific information governance policies that all employees are required to follow. An employee handbook is an important part of maintaining awareness. Once received, regular updates and changes need to be communicated as the company grows and new threats are realized. The employee manual should be given to each employee when they start their employment, and they should be required to review and sign that they understand. The manuals can be a part of the ongoing employee training, but always have employees verify with a signature that they are aware of changes. When issues arise, the solution is in writing and has been agreed upon by both employee and employer. Good agreements make for good relationships, and an employee manual goes a long way toward putting everyone— management, employees, and stakeholders—on the same page. When employees do not comply with the information governance best practices, employees will increase the risk of data breach and the cybersecurity risk to both the employees and organization. Providing this information regularly assists in protecting both your employees and your business.

## INTERNET AND ONLINE ACCESS

Internet and online access protocols not only protect the business but can protect the employee as well. The more employees understand this, the better protected your business will be. When explaining this to employees, they should be given an understanding of what constitutes PII and company confidential information. They should be concerned with things like passwords, e-mail addresses, Social Security numbers, client lists and their PII, and business plans among many, many others.

Most people seem to struggle with the "why" when it comes to online security. Giving them real-case examples and an understanding of why the rules makes sense can help to instill a culture that builds on the policy foundation. Employees should have at least a cursory understanding of the threats and how following the policies can have a positive impact on the business. Applying similar policies at home can benefit and protect them personally. Before providing personal information to anyone, employees should verify that they are a trusted source. For example, a bank would not send out personal inquiries by e-mail, so if someone is seeking business or personal information, employees should ask why the information is being requested.

A simple yet often times ignored rule is to ban employees from changing or eliminating software or hardware systems put into place to protect the business. In addition, although web browsing is an important resource for research and communicating with clients. there are many threats on the web that can be encountered during everyday browsing. Safe browsing is something that includes not just technical security but good practices. Businesses should have an Internet usage policy that clearly explains to employees what they can and cannot do when using business systems to connect to the Internet as well as why this is important.

Every business needs to educate its employees about the content of the organization's Internet usage policy. Providing the information is important but ensuring understanding is more so. Employers should provide ongoing security awareness by regularly communicating with employees about safe browsing practices. Companies need to explain to employees some basics, such as how to check the URL of websites they are visiting in order to avoid visiting dangerous website. They also need to know which sites are particularly dangerous and why people should not click on most links within websites.

## Password Management

Passwords are used to protect access to business information and online tools. If employees are not careful, however, others can use their passwords to access important business and personal files and information, and even gain entry into the network and take control. Common security problems with the use of passwords in businesses include employees writing their passwords down and posting them in places where others can see them, keeping a file on their computer labeled "passwords" that contains all other passwords, or even sharing passwords. As was stated earlier, when an employee loses control of their password it becomes very difficult to determine who is accessing the system, which leaves not just the system and the data but also the employee in jeopardy. A robust password system should be implemented that makes it difficult to steal passwords and forces the use of more passwords that are difficult to crack. Many employees do not change their passwords on a regular basis, which is another very important part of a policy that needs to be automated to drive the change. Password security is an important of part of both personal and business security. Changing the culture of the enterprise to include a focus on passwords is a great first step at changing the overall culture toward a more security minded business.

Every business should have a password policy. Both businesses and employees should consider the following when creating a strong password:

- Avoid common words such as *password* and avoid simple sequences of numbers such as 1234.
- Avoid easy-to-guess personal names, such as a child's first name.
- Create passwords that are at least eight characters in length. The more characters that are used the better. Some financial and defense contractor companies require 14–20 character passwords. Utilize special characters when possible and not just numbers and letters.

Employees can create strong passwords by including a combination of uppercase and lowercase letters, numbers, and special characters (e.g., !, $, #, or %).

Businesses need to explain to employees that strong passwords are the baseline for data security and that they are important to their personal online security as well as the business's security. It should be mandated for employees in the business environment and highly encouraged in their personal lives. Some rules that should always be incorporated into a strong password policy:

- Keep passwords confidential.
- Change passwords regularly. Your business should require employees to change their login passwords at least every three months.
- Avoid use of the same password for multiple accounts or systems.

Additionally, consider using a password manager (a program that generates and stores random passwords) that takes the creation of passwords out of the employee hands and creates very strong passwords.

## SOCIAL ENGINEERING

As we have previously discussed, social engineering takes place when someone manipulates an individual in order to obtain information about a business, its computer systems, or individuals within the business. Criminals use social engineering in order to gather the information they need to commit fraud, to steal, or to gain access to or control of computer systems. Normally, they will seem to be credible and often times helpful. They may claim they have a legitimate connection to the business or with another employee. Some will impersonate the government in order to use fear to get what they want. They will often ask for or demand information such as phone numbers or account information, or have the employee open e-mails with attachments. Sometimes this ploy can go completely unrecognized. Sometimes it is figured out but usually after the fact when the damage is already done. These tactics are popular because they work. It is important for employees to know how social engineering works and always to verify identity before giving any information.

Through policy changes, cultural changes, and training, employees will become more suspicious of any phone calls, visits, or e-mail messages from individuals asking about employees, their families, or the business. The idea that there are individuals and groups that look to manipulate and take advantage of people's good nature is often times hard to fathom. Citing real-world examples and having experts talk and teach can help to reinforce how important being suspicious is. This all should be part of your ongoing security training. Ask employees to verify the identity of anyone suspicious. When in doubt, ask a supervisor or a colleague for help. Likewise, employees should always report any suspicious activity—including actual or perceived social engineering attempts—to a supervisor.

As your employees increase their awareness, you may have issues brought to your attention. Your reaction should be to safeguard those assets that may be targeted and to ensure that others within the organization are aware. Additionally, contacting law enforcement may help to stop the events from happening again.For example, if there is reason to believe your business banking information may have been released or stolen, contact your bank immediately and ask them to help you secure your accounts. It could even mean closing your accounts and opening new ones. If the breach involved or was suspected to involve employee or customer PII, contact law enforcement and a provider of data breach notification and remediation. You may have a legal obligation to notify those whose information was impacted.

## SOCIAL MEDIA

A social media policy will provide a detailed explanation and clarification for all employees and vendors on what company information and/or issues can be discussed within and outside the business. This policy should include basic tenants and the negative impact on both the company and employee if this policy is ignored—either accidentally or on purpose. Social media policy components should include:

- Disclosure of employee identity when representing the company;
- Honesty and transparency in all communications;
- Consistency on all social media platforms;
- Prohibiton of flaming or bashing, which can result in hostile Internet interaction;
- Prohibition of paying anyone outside the business to write an endorsement;
- Employee education and training specific to social media policy changes and updates; and
- Employee and employer protocols for any crisis-related event.

Social networking sites like Facebook, Twitter, and LinkedIn can be excellent tools for your business to reach potential customers and build stronger relationships with clients. But social networking sites are becoming a popular way for cybercriminals to try to exploit the information they provide to get your personal or business information in order to hack into your personal or business computer systems. If your business uses social networking sites for marketing or professional purposes, we recommend that a dedicated individual (or group of individuals) be appointed to post content in your business's name.

Social networking should be addressed in your business's Internet usage policy Here are some social networking recommendations that you should consider:

- Be clear on what information about your business can be posted and who is authorized to do so.
- Do not post sensitive business information in the business profile or your personal posts.
- Be careful using applications on social networking sites. Many of these come from third parties and may have malware installed or may not be secure. Always check on the application provider before downloading

- When communicating through social media, be suspicious of any messages that ask for sensitive business information or about employees and their families. Be suspicious of requests to link to people that you do not know.
- Think before you post. Posts to social media sites are generally permanent and even if not, others can take screen shots to make them permanent. The basic rule is if you post a comment or a picture it is available forever. You cannot pull it back.

While at work, your employees are also likely to use social media for personal reasons. Social media is part of the fabric or most people's lives and it needs to be recognized as such. It is important that employees follow similar guidelines to protect their own information when using social networks. These guidelines will protect them personally and your business's networks and devices as well.

## SENSITIVE INFORMATION

Handling sensitive information requires employees to use discretion and confidentiality and your business to have systems and procedures in place to ensure that sensitive information is kept secure. The sensitive information could be customer or employee PII, internal business or financial records, or business plans. The loss, misuse, or modification of this type of data could result in irreparable hardship to your business. It is not just the loss of the data that causes harm; it is also the reputational impact, the revenue loss, and the litigation and regulatory issues that may result.

Some recommendations for handling sensitive employee and customer information include:

- When important or confidential information is not being used, keep it locked up and restrict access. With digital information the best means of securing the data is by keeping it safe physically as well as protecting it with encryption and limiting access. Keep paper documents under lock and key, preferably in a fire safe. Sensitive information should always be labeled as such whether in paper form or digital form. This naming convention should go across all digital formats. Digital information can be grouped by category and level of sensitivity, and stored together in a specific database. Employees should be trained in proper handling.
- A data retention policy is a part of any information governance program. The policy should specify how to properly dispose of all types of files, electronic as well as paper.
- Storage media should be wiped and then physically destroyed. Don't just throw out an old hard drive; drill a hole in the case to destroy the platters to ensure it is completely unrecoverable.
- When destroying paper records, use a high-quality cross-cut shredder or professional documents destruction company.

- Anyone working remotely should only work on sensitive data when using a VPN.
- Have clear and defined access limits for people, particularly contractors and those working remotely. Monitor their access.
- When working remotely, everyone should be utilizing a secure wireless system as well as the VPN.
- While traveling avoid the use of public or unknown wireless connections.

Working remotely is a requirement in most businesses today. There is great value from a productivity standpoint, and with proper care and planning it can be done effectively and safely. A good information governance program promotes that care and planning. The implementation needs to be evaluated regularly, as this can be a very vulnerable area for any business.

## Tablets and Smartphones

Devices such as tablets and smartphones offer new and exciting functionality. These devices are mini-computers that can be used to manipulate and store data much like a full-size computer. Due to the incredible features and abilities of these machines, they can be the means by which cybercriminal steal information or users make mistakes and release data when they shouldn't.

Due to the portability they also are easily misplaced and stolen fairly often. With the power and storage capability they have, they need to be managed very closely. Users need to understand their significance. If they are stolen or compromised and not encrypted or locked, the consequences to your business can be significant. Many phones have a direct pipe to the network, and if that falls into the wrong hands, the results would not be good.

The following recommendations will help you decrease the risk of losing data from mobile devices:

- Smartphones and tablets should have the same or more stringent security requirements as laptops due to their size and propensity to be lost or stolen. Activate the settings that auto-lock the phone or tablet when not used for a short amount of time.
- Utilize available encryption capability for e-mails.
- Back up your device contents on a regular basis.
- Ensure that security such as anti-virus software is installed on the device.
- When a phone or tablet is stolen, it should be reported to the police. Be certain to retain the serial number of each device so it can easily be handed over to the authorities. Additionally, install or activate tracking on the device so if lost it can be located. Finally, load software that enables a system administrator to wipe the device remotely. This is particularly important in the event of the device disappearing or an employee being discharged.

## PORTABLE DATA STORAGE

Technology today has developed to the point that enormous amounts of data can be stored on portable devices. Portable hard drives can hold terabytes of information. So much data can be stored on these pieces of equipment that you may be able to store all the data from your business on a single hard drive. While DVDs and CDs are still used, they have for the large part been replaced. USB devices such as flash drives and external hard drives have taken over. The cost and convenience of portable devices is excellent. There are issues, however. The risk of infection by a virus or malware is high, particularly with flash drives. Due to their very nature (small and portable) they can be lost or stolen easily, and they can be targeted by cybercriminals. In one case, a criminal dropped several USB flash drives loaded with malware into a parking lot of a large company hoping someone would pick one up and plug it into a company computer. It worked.

There are a few simple rules to follow when dealing with portable storage devices.

- Only use devices that have encryption capability to store sensitive or PII data.
- Have clear rules for what data can be stored on what devices. Train your employees on the proper use and control of each device.
- Properly label each device with the company name and contact information.
- Properly dispose of older devices

## EMPLOYEE SECURITY

An information governance policy has a duty to ensure that the business is hiring and managing employees in a fair and equitable manner, while making certain that those hired are honest and trustworthy. Additionally, a system of ongoing vigilance and recurring evaluation needs to be in place to maintain a high level of integrity within the work group.

A few of the items to consider implementing in your policies are below. Please keep in mind that management should always consult with human resources and legal when it comes to employee issues. Information governance is designed to help promote a better work environment. Poorly written policies and procedures can result in legal and personnel issues, so make sure they are written property.

- Include in your employee manual a section on information security. Make sure it spells out what employees are allowed to do and what they are not. Included should be the repercussions if a data breach is the fault of an employee. Pre-employment background checks are an absolute must. Likewise, there are pre-employment integrity tests that are available to verify that you are hiring people who can be trusted. Most businesses never screen employees again, but it is important to recognized that situations change and employees can have events in their lives that should preclude them from having access to your data. It is a good idea to do annual background checks on anyone that has access to your confidential data. This can often be a condition of employment.

- All employees must sign—and should re-sign annually—noncompetition, non-disclosure, intellectual property agreements, and other contractual agreements that are necessary for their jobs.
- All employees as a condition of employment should have to be trained and sign an agreement regarding their security responsibilities. Additionally, all contractors should have to go through the same training and sign off.
- Finally, business must clearly communicate the consequences and follow through on any actual event. Not following through with accountability can lead to a lax attitude regarding cybersecurity as well as security in general.

## TERMINATION OF AN EMPLOYEE

One of the more dangerous times from a cybersecurity standpoint is the termination of an employee. There are many documented cases of damage and theft being done to networks just before and right after being fired. Letting go of an employee is never easy, but taking proper steps to secure your network and data is vital.

Keep in mind that dismissing contractors can have similar dangers. Information technology employees and contractors are particularly difficult. A few helpful hints:

- Lockout the employee or contractor from accessing the network immediately upon notification they are leaving or while you are discharging them.
- Collect all company owned devices and computers from them, even phones. They should not be allowed to wipe the hard drives.
- Make a forensic image of any device you intend to repurpose.
- Inform a more senior and trusted IT person of the discharge and have them verify that the person no longer has access to the network

## KEY WORDS, PHRASES, AND DEFINITIONS

An understanding of key words, phrases, and definitions are important in order for the employer to be able to support employee education and awareness. These key words, phrases, and definitions will serve as a point of reference to current and future information governance objectives.

According to the Privacy Rights Clearinghouse, which is a California-based non-profit consumer organization that tracks and reports on privacy and security laws along with publicly known data breach events, there are eight types of data breaches including:[5]

- Unintended disclosure (DISC): Sensitive information posted publicly on a website, mishandled, or sent to the wrong party via e-mail, fax, or mail.
- Hacking or malware (HACK): Electronic entry by an outside party, malware, and spyware.

- Payment Card Fraud (CARD): Fraud involving debit and credit cards that is not accomplished via hacking, such as skimming devices at point-of-service terminals.
- Insider (INSD): Someone with legitimate access—such as an employee or contractor—intentionally breaches information.
- Physical loss (PHYS): Lost, discarded, or stolen nonelectronic records, such as paper documents.
- Portable device (PORT): Lost, discarded, or stolen laptop, PDA, smartphone, portable memory device, CD, hard drive, data tape, etc.
- Stationary device (STAT): Lost, discarded, or stolen stationary electronic device such as a computer or server not designed for mobility.
- Unknown or other (UNKN).

In addition, the following definitions of identity theft, types of identity theft, types of scams, and identity theft resources will help employees support their information governance objectives.

- Consumer Identity Theft: The FTC defines "identity theft" as a fraud that is committed or attempted use of a person's identifying information without authority. In essence, if you use someone else's information to benefit yourself, you are committing identity theft.
- Personally Identifiable Information: PII is data that are used to identify an individual. Think of Social Security numbers, addresses, names, and contact information.
- Personal Privacy: Your personal information is more than just your PII as defined above. It is your activity that is tracked such as medical information, employment history, and shopping habits. Everyone has a right to the privacy of this information. The theft and misuse of it is illegal.
- Password Management: Password management is the effective use of the most basic of security measures. As we stated earlier, using weak or easily defeated passwords is unacceptable and bad for business.
- Child ID Theft: This is a fast growing segment of the identity theft world. It has become popular because most parents do not even realize the theft has occurred until the child needs to establish credit for a job or school.
- Criminal ID Theft:This type of identity theft occurs in relation to a crime. If someone successfully uses your identity when receiving a traffic ticket or even is arrested for a felony it goes on your record. If the person gets out on bail, it becomes your responsibility to clear your name.
- Employment Fraud ID Theft: Employment fraud is when someone uses your Social Security number and good credit and background to gain employment. This become bad news at tax time for the victim.
- Financial ID Theft: The most known and recognized form of identity theft. Someone steals your identity in an effort to get credit or open fraudulent bank accounts.

- Governmental Benefits ID Theft: Another type of theft designed to gain access to benefits provided to another, such as social security, welfare, or unemployment.
- Medical Benefits ID Theft: Also known health record identity theft. This is the fastest growning form of identity theft. This occurs when someone uses another persons health records to obtain medical care. Medical records are now mandated to be digital by 2016 and as such will become more portable. Think of a health record victim having an emergency procedure in another state and due to the ID theft the physician pulls up the wrong data. This takes identity theft from a financial loss to a serious health concern...or worse. You can also end up getting a medical bill for services you did not receive.
- Senior ID Theft: Another growing concern. Seniors are vulnerable and often are not as aware of the threats in technology.
- Social Media ID Theft: This is often a means to an end. Social media information is stolen and used to social engineer someone else to gain access to a company or a network.
- Synthetic ID Theft: By utilizing fake identities to come up with a brand new identity thieves can avoid detection and still reap the benefits. This can be much more difficult to perpetrate but it can also be very lucrative.
- Cybercrime: In today's world the criminals are learning that cybercrime is easier and more profitable than traditional crime. Cybercrime is using electronic means to steal information or other items. As technology has become more pervasive cyber crime has followed suit.
- Pharming: The process of redirecting Internet domain name requests to false websites to collect personal information.
- Phishing: The use of e-mail to get victims to provide confidential information. Spear phishing is the same scam but targeted at one individual. This is what we think of when we think of spammers.
- Skimming: Some thieves will steal debit or credit card information by using a skimmer. These devices record all the card's information, which can be used to make fraudulent cards. Skimmers that look identical to the actual ATM card slot can also be attached to the front of ATMs.
- Spoofing: Spoofing is where a fake website is developed in order to collect PII that unsuspecting victims provide through the use of Spyware which, is a virus that is downloaded onto a computer without the owner's knowledge. It can either cause damage or collect and transmit PII.
- Vishing or Voice Phishing: This scam involves sending an e-mail in hopes of getting victims to call a voice mailbox to disclose sensitive financial and personal information.

According to an August 2011 Digital Forensic Association (DFA) report, *The Leaking Vault: Six years of Data Breaches*, the DFA found that in the past six years an average of 388,000 records per day were lost or stolen, approximately 15,000 records per hour were lost or stolen. We need to be prepared. We need to be aware. We need to have systems in place to combat the threats that are changing and evolving. A solid information governance program can give you the base for protecting your business, but it needs to be in the fabric of the organization. Everyone must buy in and senior leadership needs to lead the way.

## References

1.  2013 Verizon Data Breach Investigations Report, April 2013, accessed December 1, 2013. http://www.verizonenterprise.com/resources/reports/rp_data-breach-investigations-report-2012-ebk_en_xg.pdf.
2.  Ponemon Institute, *2013 Cost of Data Breach Study: Global Analysis* (Ponemon Institute, 2013), accessed October 1, 2013. http://www.ponemon.org/local/upload/file/2013%20Report%20GLOBAL%20CODB%20FINAL%205-2.pdf.
3.  Kelly Jackson Higgens, "No 'One Size Fits All' In Data Breaches, New Verizon Report Finds," *Dark Reading Magazine*, April 22, 2013, accessed November 2, 2013. http://www.darkreading.com/attacks-breaches/no-one-size-fits-all-in-data-breaches-new-verizon-report-finds/d/d-id/1139583?.
4.  National Cyber Security Alliance, Symantec, and JZ Analytics, *2012 NCSA/Symantec National Small Business Study* (2012), accessed November 2, 2013. https://www.staysafeonline.org/download/datasets/4389/2012_ncsa_symantec_small_business_study.pdf.
5.  Privacy Rights Clearinghouse, accessed November 5, 2013. https://www.privacyrights.org/data-breach-how-to.

# Chapter 6

# The Human Element

Human beings are inherently unique, and it is this uniqueness that makes it difficult to predict what people will do. This is the problem with humans when it comes to information governance. Controlling behaviors and mitigating bad behavior is just another reason for establishing clear information governance policies and procedures.

Any business dealing with personal information could face serious consequences if employees fail to keep their clients' information from the public, predators, or anyone who could misuse the information. Companies dealing with intellectual property will need to keep their employees from talking about their projects with anyone outside of the company. Excited employees who want to share what they are doing with family could accidentally leak secret parts of a story or schematic. Inadvertently starting a rumor could jeopardize the company's project, product, or presentation. Sharing plot details for a television show or movie could spoil the experience if the details were revealed and posted on the Internet.

When addressing the human role, information governance has been described as "the specification of decision rights and an accountability framework to encourage desirable behavior in the valuation, creation, storage, use, archival and deletion of information."[1] Note the focus on the "desirable behavior" of the employees when handling the information of an organization. Information governance involves many procedures that can be difficult to implement in the work place and must be meticulously planned. An organization must identify by whom, for what, why, and how information will be used. If successful in implementing and maintaining the effort, the business can mitigate risks while operating efficiently. A good information governance plan that accounts for the individuality of humans can not only ensure a business will survive in the modern era but can help the business thrive as well.

Although they can be exception to every rule, employees will not always benefit the organizations for which they work. For a host of reasons—lack of proper training, unhappiness, criminal intent—employees are at the root of most problems surrounding compromises of information. As mentioned in chapter one, we need look only so far as Edward Snowden, the self-described whistleblower who allegedly took thousands of electronic documents from the NSA and has shared with those who are not necessarily allies of the United States. National security issues aside, the purported acts of Mr. Snowden have vastly changed the way in which much of the world views America's government in general and the NSA in particular.

So how exactly do employees affect information governance? It all depends upon what policies have been put into place and what has been done to ensure employees are following these policies.

# Cyber

Cyber security is a major concern when it comes to the human element of information governance. After all, most records are electronic, and humans are operating the computers and all the other electronic equipment necessary for companies to operate. Let's take a look at some of the common pitfalls that are present when human beings are handling sensitive information.

## SOCIAL ENGINEERING

As we have reiterated throughout the book, the major concern is about companies having their sensitive information unnecessarily released to others who should not have access. Once of the most common forms of unintentionally releasing information is through social engineering.

Social engineering used to be all about saying the right things to an employee who could be unwittingly duped. As human beings, it is our tendency to want to help. Someone calls a company and tells the employee they have lost the information that had been sent to them and asks could they please resend it. The caller knows the right things to say and usually has a few names of company executives to mention in order to add credibility to the request. Part of the theme in social engineering is to create a sense of urgency (e.g., "I have to have this information immediately for the boss!").

As technology has grown, social engineering has moved from contact in-person and over the telephone to the computer screen. Keeping information properly hidden from those who do not have clearance has never been more challenging. The less tech-savvy your employees, the more susceptible they are to social engineering.

The attack could be in the form of an e-mail with a link to a nefarious website that infects the corporate computer with malware. Or perhaps someone in the organization has posted their résumé on a job search website, listing their position in the company and the specific projects they are work on. This could allow someone posing as a potential employer to conduct an interview for more details; details they hope will include information they can use.

Those in charge of information governance must make sure good employees understand how easy it is for social engineering to jeopardize vital information. They also need to ensure proper training has been provided so that information is stored securely and according to company policy. With the proper education and training, good employees can make information governance a solid barrier between your organization and those who would do your company harm.

## Passwords

Another example of an employee not practicing good security measures would be the use of a simple password. Most employees do not fully appreciate the nuances of computer security, so they use simple passwords that are easy to remember. Unfortunately, a simple password makes it simple for a hacker to break into the system or for a social engineer to obtain. This affects information governance because it heightens the risk of security breach.

Although we wish for employees to use more complex passwords, we likewise do not want them to have to write their passwords down, as doing so will create a situation where this information might be discovered by someone who will have nefarious intentions. Instead, the key is to educate employees on how to create a complex password that is easy to remember.

A basic formula for a complex password that is easy to remember uses dates that are familiar to the individual, such as the year of their wedding or the birth of their children. These are then strung together in such a way that compromising the password would be virtually impossible.

Let's say, for example, that an employee has two children, one born in the year 2000 and the other in 2005. Combining these numbers into a password it might look something like this:

$$2000plus2005 = 4005$$

This creates a password that utilizes numbers, upper and lower case letters, and symbols, all combined in a way that is easy to remember. Additionally, this password formula can be individualized for each different program the user accesses by adding a simple extension to the end. For example for Facebook the password might look like 2000plus2005 = 4005FB. For a LinkedIn account it would look like 2000plus2005 = 4005LI. The password formula is simple enough for all employees to comprehend yet provides a high level of strength to address security concerns.

## INTERNET USE

In today's world almost every employee has access to the Internet at work. But what your employees are actually doing on the Internet can present a threat to your company.

The first consideration is whether your company has an Internet usage policy for its employees. From a standpoint of productivity alone, you probably don't want your employees surfing the internet or updating their Facebook profiles all day long. There is nothing wrong with affording some Internet leisure time during the day, but having general guidelines for use can ensure that employees do not become overly distracted from their work.

The next issue related to Internet usage occurs when employees access their social media, whether it be at work or home. What are they saying about the business? Disparaging comments about the company can easily go viral and negatively impact the company's reputation. Furthermore, employees posting openly about ongoing projects can reveal to competitors your business opportunities. For example, you would not want an employee telling someone about your next million-dollar venture via a Facebook post. A solid information governance policy should take into consideration social media use both on and off the job.

Finally, visiting unapproved websites offers the possibility of inadvertently downloading malicious software to your company's computer system. Many companies have policies in place regarding the use or distribution of both personal and corporate information. Access to information is easier today, as most organizations have implemented internal computer systems along with their Internet access. As a result, if an employee does not make sure the data are "accurate, protected and easily managed, companies are losing millions of dollars in avoidable costs."[2] In addition, accuracy, ability, and privacy are hard to manage as the "storage requirements are doubling every 19 months."[3]

The use of the Internet allows an employee to knowingly or unknowingly share sensitive information if they are careless about entering data, share their passwords, disregard security measures, leave their laptops or tablets unprotected, or leave computer screens unlocked. Once a company's information is compromised losses are incurred in a variety of ways, including loss of customers and reduced client loyalty. Internet usage policies, along with software filters to block access to unapproved sites, can pay huge dividends in keeping your company safe and secure.

## THUMB DRIVES AND LAPTOPS

An employee's use of something as small as a thumb drive or as commonplace as a laptop can have serious consequences for an organization if not properly regulated by an information governance policy. Today thumb drives are as common in the office as pens and paper. But unlike pens and paper, thumb drives are often used to store sensitive data as it is moved from one computer to another. It is the use and transportation of thumb drives, the very purpose for which they are designed, that raises several issues of concern.

To mitigate the potential for human error, the information governance plan should address the issue of thumb drives by limiting their use by employees to only devices issued by the company. The policy should also stipulate that they may only be used on company machines. You do not want your employee plugging a company thumb drive into their personal computer or, worse yet, the computer of a third party. Despite all of the malware filters and other precautions your company has taken, it can all be undone by an employee inadvertently installing malware or spyware on the corporate system because their thumb drive was exposed on another system. Never should a thumb drive be plugged into a hotel computer while on business travel. Companies know their competitors travel for business, so it is not uncommon to find spyware loaded onto computers that hotels offer their guests. When using a thumb drive on someone else's computer, you are not just using their computer; you are using every other computer to which that computer has been linked.

It is human nature that when we find something we believe has been lost, we wish to return it to its rightful owner. If an employee finds a thumb drive in the company parking lot, the tendency is to plug it in with hopes of locating the owner. But what if that thumb drive had been purposely placed in your company's parking lot for the very purpose of downloading spyware onto your system? Employees need to be educated about these dangers. The proper procedure would be to turn any found thumb drives into the IT staff for examination on a computer system that is not connected to the company's network.

Like thumb drives, laptops also are a modern day business convenience that can pose potential corporate threats. Most laptops issued by companies carry within them sensitive information. Because humans can be careless, the information governance policy must also address how the laptop is used and maintained.

If employees bring a laptop home from work, it should never be left in the car, even for a short period of time and especially not overnight. When traveling, laptops need to be either with the employee at all times or remain locked in a hotel safe. Every day, laptops are stolen from the back seats of cars, from hotel rooms, or at conferences while employees are distracted. The laptop can easily be replaced, but it may be more difficult to replace the information it contained. One laptop containing the personal information of thousands of individuals that was stolen from an employee of the Department of Veterans Affairs resulted in the government having to pay $20 million to settle a class action lawsuit.[4] If the government can be held accountable, certainly so can the private sector.

The information governance policy on laptops should also address how they are used when traveling overseas. Foreign governments, even those friendly to the United States, have been long known to seek proprietary information from business people traveling to their countries. There have been recorded events of computers being forensically analyzed while the traveler is passing through customs. After all, with the help of their government, it is a lot easier for a foreign business to steal our trade secrets rather than invent their own technology. For this same reason, laptops should never be left behind unattended in a foreign hotel.

As a general rule, when traveling with a laptop either domestically or abroad, it is a good idea to use a machine that has limited corporate information on the hard drive, if any at all. Better to carry this information securely on a thumb drive, which can be plugged in and accessed as needed.

## ENCRYPTION

If your company routinely encrypts its important information, that's great. If not, you should think about doing so. By encrypting data that is being transported on a thumb drive or laptop, you lessen the potential for damage if the information lost or stolen. Encrypting data transmitted over networks can be an added layer of protection. This encryption removes the human element to a certain degree; an element prone to improper handling of data during the transfer, creation, and deletion of information.[5]

## Physical Acts

While cyber losses of sensitive data are of a major concern, statistically they account for only about 30 percent of all compromises. The importance of this chapter lies in the fact that the other 70 percent of the losses of sensitive information are a direct result of human interactions with other humans.

## EMPLOYEE BACKGROUNDS

In today's society most employees work for companies for the paycheck and—it is to be hoped—because they enjoy their work. Employees are the lifeblood of companies without whom the mission of the organization could not be accomplished. It a symbiotic relationship, much of which relies on trust of one another. Employees trust they will be compensated for their efforts, and companies trust their employees will perform the work as agreed.

Part of this trust equation assume that those in supervision have empowered their employees with access to a myriad of aspects of the business, most notably assets and information. With demands of data production and retention increasing, the trust that companies need to place upon their employees is continuing to grow exponentially. But as these demands continue to grow and employees are afforded greater access to sensitive data, employers must have the necessary confidence in their workforce to sustain the necessary level of trust. Pre-employment screening of various degrees (depending upon the level of access and security required) should be part of your company's information governance plan.

As was stated in Chapter 1 and according to Mark Pribish, vice president of Merchants Information Solutions, a company that conducts integrity test for new hires, "one in eight employees will present a threat to their employer at some point during the term of their employment." Pribish goes on to say that at some point in their career, an employee who does not possess a high level of integrity may become disgruntled and act upon their feeling of dissatisfaction by taking it out on the company. Their acts could include purposeful disclosure or destruction of sensitive information. Of course, these rogue employees are not only hurting the company; they are hurting their fellow employees and the victims of the disclosures and destruction as well.

In many ways information governance involves a certain level of trust. You must be able to trust employees if you expect them to help the company succeed. This is the reason companies have to be so careful when hiring potential employees for positions that require a high level of security discretion. Companies can use a variety of personality tests, background checks, and other miscellaneous examinations to evaluate whether a potential future employee would hurt or help your company. If an employee is trusted to be diligent in protecting the company's best interests, an information governance system of protocols and procedures will help the employee succeed in this mission.

## LACK OF INFORMATION GOVERNANCE EDUCATION

Many of the things already discussed in this chapter revolve around an employee knowing what to do and what not to do. Although some actions are not necessarily intuitive, none of the tasks that support a good information governance policy are overly complex.

Education must be a fundament basis of the employee's initial training, and it should be continued on a regular basis throughout their employment. A well-informed employee who has been educated to the dangers and the solutions is far less likely to create issues that threaten information than those who have not.

In most companies, the average employee will not be techno-savvy beyond what they use in everyday life. They may know how to operate a computer but think little about the pre-installed software designed to protect them. Good computer security practices are learned behavior, as are the behaviors to ensure physical security. As technology and physical issues change, so must the training. Training—at least on an annual basis but preferably more frequently—should be incorporated into your information governance protocols to ensure all employees are striving to protect the organization. If a company takes the time and spends the money on training their employees, it will not only prevent loss of information but have the added benefit of improving the efficiency of the organization across the board.

Additionally, management should be assigned the responsibility of monitoring their employees' adherence to information governance security policies. Once again, it is human nature that, despite the best of intentions, people will become complacent over time unless they have a reason to be more vigilant. Obscurity through security is not the answer. Just because employees do not see a threat does not mean that a threat is not present. Therefore, rather than have your employees become more vigilant by responding to loss of sensitive information that could have been prevent through good information governance security practices, have management delegated to monitor their compliance in order to ensure such an event does not occur in the first place.

## NOT FOLLOWING POLICIES

Once employees have been properly educated, they need to follow the organization's procedures. Although procedures are set in place to avoid risk—and despite being educated about these risks—a certain percentage of people will elect to disregard the procedures.

Employees fail to follow information governance procedures for a variety of reasons. They may find that the rules are too taxing, take too long, or are more difficult to implement than actually dealing with a compromise. An example of this would be an employee failing to properly document that they have physically removed data from storage, even though they have the authority to do so. The procedure might be for them to document what was taken along with their name, employee identification number, and the time. If an employee decides to forego documenting this removal because it is too time consuming or they plan to replace the data quickly, the information governance process has been corrupted. Furthermore, once an employee feels comfortable foregoing the process, it is unlikely they will adhere to it in the future.

As important as it is for employees to adhere to established information governance policies, it is equally as important for these policies to be correctly managed. If employees who are in supervisory positions recognize that there is a risk— whether it be personal, hardware or software related, or any other possibility—but fail to report and address violations, the corruption of the information governance policies is deepened. Such negligence on the part of supervisors also provides subordinates with tacit authority to ignore policies, believing that violations of are not of significant importance.

Because the IT staff of a company is generally small in comparison to other departments within an organization, it unrealistic to hold IT accountable for all violations of IT security that may be committed by an employee. Information security is much more than just IT. Rather, everyone in the organization should have a role when it comes to enforcement of the policies.

Employees should be empowered to report violations to management, and management should be empowered and accountable to act. Likewise, the management response to violations should not initially be punitive but rather a reiteration of the importance of the policy and the implementation of further education when necessary. Repeated acts of information governance policy violations by the same offender, however, must be considered in the context of the data integrity of the organization. When reiteration and education prove to be ineffective, management must also consider availing themselves of the tools of discipline, up to and including termination. When an individual acts in such a way that they put the company at risk but fail to correct their ways, the company needs to decide whether this particular employee is worth incurring that risk.

## NOT FOLLOWING LAWS

Policies of a company are generally self-developed and self-imposed. However, businesses also have to follow government-mandated regulations when handling certain types of information. No single law in the United States provides a comprehensive treatment of data protection or privacy issues.[6] Additionally, there have been a number of laws and executive orders dealing specifically with data protection.[7] The rules and regulations define procedures that must be followed in order to ensure that PII is properly secured and outline financial penalties for failure to do so.

## NEGLIGENCE

In some cases, the failure to adhere to information governance policies may be unintentional but of negligence none the less. An employee might leave their computer station unlocked and not shut down for the evening while the cleaning crew services the building, negligently affording the opportunity for prying eyes to take a look at the contents of the hard drive. Or an employee might have left their company smart phone behind at a restaurant, providing full access to the corporate contacts—including home phones numbers—creating an enhanced opportunity for criminals to gather information through social engineering. No matter the type of negligence, an information governance policy that clearly outlines steps each employee is responsible to take helps mitigate potential negligent acts.

## DISGRUNTLED EMPLOYEES

Remember the statistic that one out of eight employees will become disgruntled during their work life and may act against his or her company? Human beings sometimes form grudges against those with whom they are employed. When in the midst of a grudge, what better way is there to "get even" with a company than to make it look bad. The release of a company's sensitive data is as bad as it gets.

Disgruntled employees—whether outright hostile or simply not sufficiently dedicated to the cause—have the potential to easily share their organization's vital information. These employees may skip protocols or share security information such as passwords. Information governance is all about managing this information.

Despite having good information governance policies in place, the advent of social media and other technologies at our fingertips has made it easier than ever to release information to a large number of people with nothing more than a few strokes on a keyboard. If perhaps an employee were to release a screen shot of a product under development, the entire enterprise would be undermined before the company ever had a chance to bring their product to fruition. Even if the product was not compromised, the public might view an unfinished product and form lasting negative impressions, which could dampen the product's commercial success. This is one basic examples of why the flow of information in an organization must be controlled, not just as it moved from the company to the employee but also from the company to the public. Again, the solution is the same. Information governance policies that cover the do's and don'ts of handling important information make it easier for management to govern and taken the appropriate protective action.

## CRIMINAL ACTS

In some cases, employees' actions that violate information governance policies may actually be criminal and require law enforcement intervention. Corporate espionage on behalf of another business or an employee outright stealing proprietary information from their employer in order to make a sale to the highest bidder are just two of the examples of commonplace criminal activity that can seriously impact a company's reputation and financial security. Information governance policies are the key to enabling law enforcement to get involved.

One recent example of this types of crime involves a medium-sized company of a hundred employees that provides services to those wishing to consolidate their debts. During the height of the poor economy, this company engaged a large numbers of clients, earning the company high residuals every month as they profited on a percentage of the debt consolidation and collection. Likewise, the company was spending large sums of money on a monthly basis—totally millions of dollars annually—in order to obtain comprehensive lists of thousands of potential clients. Several employees within the company decided to leave and start their own competing business. After giving their notice, but before parting ways, they decided to help themselves to the electronic records that contained the thousands and thousands of customer leads. They did so by accessing the company's network using their company issued passwords. In a short period of time, these new competitors put the original company out business. They were able to undercut the prices of the original company because they had not had to pay millions of dollars for the lead information.

So the police investigated, arrests were made, and everyone went to jail, right? Wrong! None of the company's employee records, documents, or procedures made reference to the handling of propriety or sensitive information. Nothing indicated this information was for the sole and specific use of the company and no one else. Without some sort of employee agreement to that effect, it was impossible to prove criminal intent in a court of law.

It might seem like common sense to the average citizen, but under the law certain legal elements need to be met. It is a comprehensive information governance policy what will facilitate meeting this need. It should be further noted that the company in question also lacked policies regulating the use of passwords and unauthorized access of the network, both of which could have prevented the poaching of the customer lead information.

## Non-Disclosure Agreements

Having a non-disclosure agreement is an easily incorporated yet important part of an information governance plan. By simply making such a document a standard practice when hiring new employees—as well as having current employees also sign such an agreement—companies can ensure that their information is legally protected from unauthorized release. A non-disclosure agreement further protects an organization by outlining applicable legal consequences should an employee purposefully leak protected information, thereby giving the company a defined means of restitution.

Despite the existence of a non-disclosure agreement, however, should a current or past employee elect to release sensitive information anyway, it is highly unlikely that they would admit to doing so. Therefore, the victim company should still anticipate having some sort of investigation conducted, either internally or through law enforcement, in an effort to establish the source of the leak before criminal actions or civil restitution could be pursued.

## Need-to-Know

Along the same lines as non-disclosure agreements concerning sensitive information is the concept of need-to-know. Extremely common in both the federal government and the military, need-to-know is being taken more and more seriously in the private sector. The concept is as simple as it sounds: if an employee does not have a need to know the information, the information should not be shared with the employee. By limiting access to employees who have a specific business reason for exposure to sensitive information, the number of employees that can compromise the information—whether by accident or on purpose—will have been minimized.

Some in the business world find the concept of need-to-know offensive, believing that employees should be trusted or they would otherwise not be employees of the company in the first place. Others speak of transparency in business and that by sharing all information with all employees every member of the company feels as if they are a vested part of the team. As noble as these ethical positions may be, the realities of information governance dictate otherwise.

A basic example would be human resources records. Almost everyone would agree that private information within an employee's file, such as pay increases or disciplinary actions, are the sole business of the employer and the employee. Employees expect privacy when it comes to this sort of information and, for that reason, companies limit access to employee files to their human resources personnel who have a need to know.

The same concept of need-to-know should be incorporated into any project that involves proprietary or sensitive information. In doing so, companies immediately add an extra layer of protection to a valuable asset by limiting the risk of unauthorized exposure.

## Code Names for Projects

Taking another idea from the government and military, comprehensive information governance plans should take into consideration policies that assign codes names for projects in development containing sensitive information that others may wish to pilfer.

When developing proprietary information or formulating significant business developments that may draw attention, assigning a code name to the project will have the effect of misdirection. In addition to the mystique of referring to a project by a different name, doing so will enable those involved to discuss the matter without concern of being overheard or inadvertently disclosing too much information. Likewise, by code-naming files, persons who gain access to a company's network—whether an internal employee or outside hacker—will not be able to readily identify files to be removed. Code-naming sensitive projects is just another way of adding a further layer of security to the overall information governance plans.

## ACCESS BADGES

Most large and medium companies along with the occasional small business use access badges that their employees wear. The badges are designed to identify visibly to others within the organization that they are employees of the company. In many cases, they will also limit access to certain areas to those employees who meet the need-to-know criterion. Although badges are a highly effective tool in controlling physical access when used properly, many employees forgo the basic protocols. Even when they have no malicious intent, their actions can end up jeopardizing information security all the same.

Once again, human nature plays a role. As human beings, it is generally in our nature to be courteous. When we use our badges to pass through a door and see another person walking toward us, our instinct is to hold the door open for the other person. In the world of physical security, these persons are known as "tailgaters." They pose a potential threat to information security—as well as to the physical security of facilities.

What if it is a large company and you do not recognize the person for whom you are holding the door? Could you be unwittingly providing access to a secure area and the information it contains by letting someone through who is using a fraudulent badge? Even if they are employees, do they have authorization to be the area in question?

The authors are not suggesting that employees suspend common courtesies to one another. Rather, when faced with a situation where you might be sure of the person's identify and the level of access they are granted, it is always better to err on the side of caution in the interest of proper information governance. This can be easily accomplished by a polite challenge to the person regarding who they are and where they work. If you are met with reluctance to be cooperative, then it is a good bet that either the person does not hold the proper access or needs a refresher in proper information governance procedures. By not only using of access badges but specifying the responsibilities of all employees to be vigilant in ensuring the authorized use of such badges, employees are empowered with specific roles in ensuring information is safely maintained. Additionally, the incorporation of specific language into the information governance plan regarding the challenging of others when deemed appropriate alleviates the hesitancy we as humans might otherwise feel.

## UPDATING POLICES

As technology changes, its use in business will change as well. For a very brief time, iPads were a novelty, but now they are found everywhere in the workplace. As changes occur, they must be covered in an information governance plan. In general, any policy that is not kept up-to-date is a weak policy that threatens security.

## COMMITTEE FOR INFORMATION GOVERNANCE

The responsibility of maintaining information governance policies should not be the job of one individual. Rather, the company should select persons from various divisions within the organization, all of whom have a stake in ensuring that PII, proprietary information, and any other type of important information is properly maintained in the best interest of the company, as well as in the interest of all who could be affected by an unauthorized release.

Logically, IT will have a role in this committee. For years, those within IT have been thought of as accountable for any breaches of information, but rarely have they had a seat at the table to discuss how to prevent these breaches. Just as importantly, it was a rare occasion when a company heeded the warnings of IT professionals and spent money on areas where no problem had occurred. The IT department has often been its own island inside large companies, overseen by managers who do not fully understand the language or importance of IT. Yet, IT departments can significantly help information governance efforts through their knowledge of threats and their ability to share this knowledge with others in the organization. But the responsibilities of information governance should no longer fall to the IT department alone.

The committee of the future for information governance should include multiple persons with multiple roles. Ideally, the committee will report directly to top management. In a perfect world, the company would have a vice president of information governance, whose role was to oversee both technological and physical security of the company's important information. In doing so, this person could report directly to the chief executive, making concerns known without having them filtered and diluted as the message passed through layers of management, perhaps never even reaching those who are in a position to take action.

This committee would also oversee the necessary training curriculum for new employees, including the company's information governance policies and how they are enforced. Likewise, this committee would have the authority to direct continued refresher training for existing members of the organization, whether through seminars, exercises, posters, fliers, or whatever means the committee decides is appropriate.

As the concerns for information governance changes, so should the makeup of the information governance committee. New members brought in at regular intervals will bring fresh thoughts and perspectives, further enabling information governance policies to continue to evolve as new technologies are produced and as business cultures continue to change.

## SUMMARY

In essence, information governance is completely reliant on employees. It is a mix of specific responsibilities combined with security needs, all of which involve humans interacting with one another. Information governance policies that are clear, specific, articulated, and frequently reviewed position employees to do well when it comes to keeping information secure. And when employees do well, companies will succeed.

## References

1.  Debra Logan, "What is Information Governance? And Why is It So Hard?" *The Gartner Blog Network*, January 11, 2010, accessed September 14, 2013. http://blogs.gartner.com/debra_logan/2010/01/11/what-is-information-governance-and-why-is-it-so-hard/.

2.  Nathaniel Rowe, *The Big Data Imperative: Why Information Governance Must be Addressed Now* (Boston, Mass.: Aberdeen Group, 2012), accessed November 19, 2014. http://aberdeen.com/Aberdeen-Library/8291/RA-big-data-governance.aspx.

3.  Ibid.

4.  www.cnn.com, January 28, 2009.

5.  Logan, "What is Information Governance?"

6.  Jean Slemmons Stratford and Juri Stratford, "Data Protection and Privacy in the United States and Europe," *Iassist Quarterly* 22, no. 3 (1998): 17.

7.  Ibid.

# Chapter 7

# The Technical Side

We live in a time that is called the Information Age, and it is well known that the information we create, store, look after, and eventually delete as consumers, employees, managers, and other roles we play in life is more than has ever been amassed before. It should come as no surprise to anyone that the technology to which we now have access not only allows us to generate this unprecedented wealth of data; it has also given us an equally impressive potential to manage all of this information. However, with great power comes great responsibility. The fact is that while many individuals have learned to use technologys securely and efficiently, and can properly work with vast amounts of information, many others do not understand or implement important safety or security practices and procedures. Prior to the advancement of technology, these practices might not have even existed.

Being security smart today is much more than just about using the computer. Everyone is also using smartphones, external hard drives, flash drives, and a multitude of other devices to relay information from one point to another. This can included anything from simply moving a PowerPoint presentation to a USB stick so that it may be carried to another room for presentation to taking home a company laptop to be able to complete a project over the weekend by accessing the company data over a VPN.

Just as technology has made it easier to transport data, it has also made it easier for people to lose data. USB drives get lost and laptops get stolen. But technology has also made it just as easy to protect your data from potential loses. Information governance plans of today should capitalize on the advances of technology to minimize potential losses or threats to data of tomorrow.

The business world is becoming more digital, and the volume of information is growing at a lightning-fast pace. As a result, we are more exposed to potential data losses every minute of the day. Hence, proper information governance is essential for businesses to remain successful. Technology can assist greatly with the implementation of information governance plans. Just as technology has brought about global markets through the creation of infrastructures, data storage, and worldwide communications, technology can also provide mechanisms to ensure these business advantages remain safe. Modern business would not exist as it does without modern technology, and modern technology is a vehicle for modern information governance policies.

## The Benefits

Information is a valuable business asset that must be properly used in accordance with each businesses' individual policies. To address their own needs, businesses must create policies that will allow employees to manage their corporate information responsibly. In business, proper information governance must make information available to those who need it without exposing the information to potential compromise. If designed properly, the information governance policies should also streamline management and reduce costs, while ensuring compliance by employees. This proper use of information governance allows companies to reduce their legal risks associated with unmanaged or inconsistently managed information, and makes the business more agile in response to a changing marketplace.[1]

Remember the days before computers? Everything was written down on paper and stored in file cabinets. Business kept this information locked up and guarded by people, alarms, or both. Once we no longer needed these reams of paper, they had to be destroyed. Shredding, burning, and other methods of disposal were both time-consuming and expensive. Technology has changed all of this and has made the mission of information governance far easier. Employee access to information can be limited based upon their need to know and the level of position they hold within the company. This same technology can also be used to monitor and record who has accessed what information. Servers log user traffic, so if something were to be compromised, the identification of the responsible party would be simple. Likewise, file deletion is also much easier. Instead of shredding and burning, files are now deleted at the touch of a button, and software can be run to make the files completely unrecoverable to prevent any attempts at espionage.

The ability to quickly and effectively manage data has been greatly beneficial to business, but it has not come without cost. The threat resides in the easy deletion and in the simple access control. Many organizations—large and small—fail to install and implement the most basic of rules and regulations. This failure leads to the possibility of disaster when the data is mismanaged. Whether intentionally or not, employees can damage data. Information governance and a strict adherence to the management of data are the best and often last lines of defense.

## ACCESS

Technology plays a huge role in assisting the implementation of information governance. More specifically, technology can fulfill the role of preventing failures in information governance from occurring. Technology can assist with information governance through the restriction of information. Passwords, file access, privilege databases, security systems, firewalls, and an assortment of other options can be used to restrict information to those who are meant to have access. Through the restriction of access, businesses can be more secure with their information, knowing that tasks involving data can be performed safely and efficiently without fear of unintended alteration or deletion.

Of course, employees must have access to information to do their jobs, but they must also be in compliance with business policies on information governance to be able to access the information needed. When employees are using information or have certain levels of access, the information should be monitored and protected by passwords, and other technological security measures should be implemented to ensure information is kept safe and used appropriately. Furthermore, access must be tracked, with logs kept in order to verify that people are accessing what they should and nothing else. Sound harsh? Not really. Let your people have access to everything they need and give them good tools to do their jobs, but remove as much of the threat or temptation as possible. Manage and empower your people but keep your data sacred. The combination of your people with the correct usage of is what will grow and sustain your business.

Technology has also greatly increased our ability to access information. The days of flipping through index cards to find a book by the Dewey Decimal System are long gone. To find publications, you can simply search through a catalog of books electronically based upon the book's title, author, or subject. In much the same way, information in the business world can be filed and retrieved, making it easier to catalog and document important and proprietary information. Employees no longer need to search through various physical records from multiple departments to find all the relevant information required to conduct business. There are no boundaries based on geography. Two employees on opposite sides of the globe can work on a document simultaneously. With a sound information governance program you not only more deeply secure your vital information but you improve effectiveness and efficiency across your enterprise.

## AUTOMATION

Automation brought about by technology has made many functions of work far less time-consuming. Whether it is the automated calculation of micro/macro metrics to determine revenue flow or assisting with the passing of information in a manner and language that can be understood by less tech-oriented individuals, automation solves problems of the business world and facilitates productivity. As data continues to grow, automation allows businesses to keep up and effectively use enormous volumes of information.

## CERTIFICATES

Certificates are another way that technology has helped information governance. This technology ensures that documents, software, and even devices are authentic. They can be used to check whether a document is genuine or whether a document or software has been modified from its original state. These certificates can also be used to ensure that only registered devices with authentic certificates can gain access to a system. This will ensure that an unauthorized user has not put an unauthorized device on a network.[2] As discussed in Chapter 3, the threat of malware in an unauthorized copy of software can be devastating to a network and the information contained within. With the advent of new technologies and software, the concept and implementation of certificates provides a level of security to the data and peace of mind to the user.

## COMMUNICATION

Electronic communication such as e-mail, text messages, faxes, and even social networking are examples of communication technology. Technology has increased the limits of communications between employees in any business. CEOs of large companies can speak with one another via the Internet from around the world. This type of networking offers somewhat secure conversations anytime, anywhere, and is practically free. Likewise, communication with employees from different locations enables companies to manage personnel from offsite, allowing companies to seek employees in areas of the world that improve cost effectiveness, while at the same time providing employment opportunities to certain regions that might not otherwise be available.

Communication technology can also be used to track employees and monitor their work production. Education sessions no longer need employers to gather everyone in one location. Rather, employees only need to view a webinar on their computer screen. Customers can receive information instantaneously. It is said that information is power, but it is more precise to say that the ability to communicate information in a timely and effective manner is power. The more we know, the more we teach, and the more we communicate, the more effective we are and the more effective our organization is. Technology is the catalyst for increased communication. Managing that flow of information is important.

## EFFICIENCY

Businesses depend on technology to help their organizations run efficiently, be competitive, and generate income. Having the ability to access vast amounts of information at any given point is incredibly beneficial. Those legitimately seeking access to information have an easier time acquiring what they need, which in turn provides greater efficiency in completing tasks. This same efficiency in the use of technology can be incorporated into the information governance plans designed to protect important data and educate employees how to do so. The efficiency achieved through technology allows security reminders to be sent to employees or remote location training opportunities to be offered. Warnings of potential dangers—such as a new malware that is downloaded via an e-mail—can be sent efficiently to employees. All of this translates into better functioning operations, which further translates into greater potentials for profitability.[3]

## ENCRYPTION

Encryption involves a method of coding files during electronic transmission and then decoding them when they are received in order to prevent sensitive information from being compromised by an unintended recipient. Businesses can use encryption to protect their assets better when sending information from one employee to another, from company to client, or from business partner to business partner.

Systems that use credit cards, debit cards, or any other kind of transaction card have encryptions in place that protect that card and PIN so that cybercriminals cannot gain access to this sensitive information. Even if a criminal manages to gain access to the system on which the card was used, the encryption is designed to prevent the criminal from being able to use this information. This makes any data that the cybercriminal obtains useless.

For instance, if a cybercriminal were to compromise a system and obtain credit card information, instead of receiving a sixteen-digit debit or credit card number like 1234-5678-9876-5432, they would instead get a what is called a hash that they would not be able to use. The hash for the previously mentioned card number could appear to be something like 522c88530c38f56f72e6cda1871e04cf. Without the proper decryption information, it is extremely difficult—if not impossible—to reverse the hash and translate it back into the credit card number. Manual attempts to reverse hashes can take months or even years.

The question that immediately comes to mind is the recent breach of the Target stores and all of their customers' credit card information. If encryption works so well, why were so many customers affected? In the case of the Target breach, the compromise was not an intrusion into the network, but rather occurred at the point of sale (POS) where the credit card is swiped. Because this was the area of the breach, the credit card information had not yet been hashed.[4] This is obviously an area of security that must be addressed, and professionals are at work developing solutions to prevent POS compromises from happening in the future.

Encryption can become a key feature of a company's information governance plan and help maintain the security of information. Like the discovery of the weakness in the Target POS compromise, more and more ways will be developed to secure information as technology continues to improve. Hence, an information governance plan has to be continually evolving, changing as new threats are discovered, and incorporating successful solutions to these threats.

## FIREWALLS

In addition to the hardware technologies available to implement information governance strategies, there is also software that can be installed on company systems to support information governance standards. One example of this is the use of firewalls. Firewalls allow certain traffic from specific ports to come into the organization's network, thus minimizing the threat of a malicious program such as a virus, worm, and Trojan back doors. Firewalls allow businesses to filter traffic by opening and closing ports so that they can better accommodate their needs.[5] These firewalls help secure the type of information to which companies wish to permit access, as well as completely blocking out malicious software.

Making sure your organization's firewall and virus protection are up to date plays a major role in the defense against cybercrimes. Employees browsing the Internet are better protected from accidentally exposing sensitive company information to those who are not authorized to view it.

## INTERNET

In terms of a technology, the Internet has had arguably more of an impact as a whole than any other type of technological development. There are few businesses today that operate without the use of the Internet in one capacity or another.

One distinct advantage of Internet use by businesses is that they can utilize off-site information storage in the form of one of the many cloud services and servers. Through the cloud, the Internet also provides businesses with ways of implementing information governance via technology by taking advantage of available integrated network systems and storing data in different locations to lower any possible collateral damage if an attack were to occur. By incorporating this basic Internet advantage into an organization's operational plans, the company has taken great strides leveraging information governance strategies.

The Internet has also streamlined and made possible many functions that otherwise would not be available. Employers can conduct a simple Google search on a perspective employee or business partner, making the organization aware of potential issues they might wish to avoid. This is a solid information governance practice that pre-empts problems before they might occur.

Likewise, the Internet connects almost the entire world and people are able to access the Internet from virtually anywhere with smartphones and tablets. This type of constant access is positive for business growth, but can also be negative when someone wants to expose information. A criminal on the other side of the globe can choose to target your business, so it is important to stay vigilant and use technology to support a business's information security.

Most individuals do not realize that they leave behind a very easily tracked trail when they surf the Internet. Those who attempt to compromise corporate information—whether by computer intrusion or an insider transferring proprietary information—make it easy to track their movements through the history of IP numbers connected to specific locations that have been recorded along the way.

By using the Internet, a completely anonymous user may be able to gain access into a database of personal information about your clients or employees. It is also much easier for a disgruntled or otherwise malicious employee to steal information from the company anonymously. But IP address information dramatically aides investigators in the discovery and capture of cybercriminals.

Additionally, these threats of stealing information via the Internet have launched a whole new area of technological development to combat these crimes. Antivirus software and employee-surveillance programs have significantly grown in the last few years, and it is easy to assume that the future will bring further advances in the arena of digital information governance.

## Managing Risk

A basic tenet of information governance is to ensure that IT will support business goals and that policies ensure compliance without needlessly restricting the company from profitable actions. Information governance policies are a way to manage risks, ensure persons understand their responsibilities and functions when it comes to securing information, and hold those not adhering to the policies accountable.

As has been addressed in this book, IT is a major stakeholder in the enforcement of these policies, but they should by no means be the only ones who have oversight. Historically, board-level executives have deferred key IT decisions to the company's IT management and business leaders. Short-term goals of those responsible for managing IT can be in conflict with the best interests of other stakeholders unless proper oversight is established. Information governance involves everyone in the system: board members, executive management, staff, customers, communities, investors, and regulators. An IT Governance structure can be used to identify and create ways to use technology in order to minimize and even mitigate risks created by this very same technology. Of course, IT must be involved in discussions involving the development of policies and procedures, but senior management should be responsible for assuring employees are adhering to the rules. Actually, it is best to have everyone affiliated with the company have some role in information governance plans, whether it is development, training, or implementation. When everyone has a stake, everyone is more interested in mitigating the risks.

These policies assist the transition from a needed action to a value on paper. For example, law and/or regulation in certain industries require record retention. Should these records be called upon by subpoena or some regulatory agency, if the company has not maintained adequate records, any number of established financial penalties could be levied against the offending organization. Information governance outlines for companies the necessary record retention policies that they must have, how they are to be followed, and for how long these records must be maintained. Further, in following the information governance policies, companies are also able to purge records in accordance with the requirements of the industry. By doing so in a manner outlined in the company policy, they have further mitigated their risks of unnecessary liability.

## PREDICTIVE CODING

One of the hardest situations for information governance is the use of unstructured data within a business, or a business that has a large amount of unstructured data through the use of shared drives, share points, and hard drives in general. While this could be handled by numerous employees with hours spent teaching them how to structure and organize data or how to go through data to get what information is needed, unstructured data can be better handled with the idea of a predictive coding system for which employees only need be trained once.

Predictive coding is a tool designed to facilitate information governance in an easier and faster manner, while improving the ease of access to files across various storage technologies and methods. Predictive coding systems are a form of computer-assisted review. Essentially, predictive coding is a series of filters through which data is passed and then sorted according to the filters' rules. This allows a technological review of the information that is much faster than would be possible if humans were to physically review documents and look for specific terms. In a business where data grows exponentially—with virtually never any reduction in the amount of data that has been collected—the manpower and resources needed to review such a vast amount of information would prove to be an extreme strain on a company's personnel resources, even if the documents were organized in a digital format. Predictive coding is established much like e-mail filters, which can be set up to sort through e-mails as they are received. In a similar manner, a proper predictive coding system will take any information and proactively file it while the information is still active. This can also be used to cut down on duplication risks as well.

When it comes to the unstructured data within networks and systems, predictive coding can be used primarily to synchronize different storage areas to allow uniformity and improve ease of access for the employees of a business. Ease of access should not be sacrificed. Rather, by incorporating predictive coding in an information governance plan, the ability to maintain and quickly locate files should become enhanced. Along this line, when information is put into a shared storage location, the information can be sorted by clients or other keyword filters whenever a document is uploaded. Likewise, one of the further benefits of this system is that when duplicates exist, a rule can be formulated to create a revision archive instead of deleting them outright, In other words, the predictive coding system would maintain a copy of the document along with copies of all previous versions.

Like any other technology, predictive coding does have its limitations. Users have to have a clear understanding of how the system works and how it can be successfully utilized within a particular organization. Also, the IT workforce will generally require a significant amount of time to implement the predicative coding in order to create the rules and goals for the system. Nevertheless, this is a small price to pay considering the amount of time that it would take to train every employee to perform these functions on the system manually, not to mention the actually overall time that will be saved by being able to store and retrieve documents so much faster. Once the system is in place, it is just a matter of determining the appropriate projects for which predictive coding can best complement an organization's business needs as well as its risk tolerance.[6] Although the predictive coding system does require a certain level of monitoring and employee instruction by the IT staff, the benefits of automating file retention along with the ability to correct any errors that might have been made makes such a system a valuable asset to any company needing to maintain a large volume of records.

## PROFITABILITY

Technology can assist the implementation of information governance through established procedures and, in many cases, the use of automation. The old business adage "time is money" has never been more true. With shrinking resources and rising prices, companies are always seeking ways to do more with less, all the while minimizing their losses. Sometimes the answer is so obvious that it is overlooked. Information governance affords businesses all of these attributes and securities, costing little in the process. It is designed to save companies time, effort, and often money by mitigating their risks.

## Recovery

Technology can greatly assist information governance plans by making it possible to recover data that might have been compromised or lost as a result of an incident. Because information governance calls for training, employees are aware of their responsibilities to help avoid loss and, likewise, may be held accountable when acts of negligence, recklessness, or malfeasance occurs. Also, companies that maintain records on a database according to their information governance polices can easily have access to backup documents should an incident occur.

In the event of a disaster—and make no mistake, losing your data is a disaster—all organizations need a way to recover their data. As with all effective policies, it comes down to planning and execution. Failing to have a recovery and backup plan and/or not being able to execute that plan are pieces that are often overlooked.

Let's think about one terrifying question. If all your data disappeared tomorrow, what would you do? If you don't know, you need to start developing a disaster recovery plan as part of your information governance program. If you do know and it scares you, you need to reevaluate. A saying that we believe applies to data breach and data loss is "It is not a matter of *if*; it is a matter of *when*."

## Security

A huge advantage of incorporating technology into your information governance planning is that it can be leveraged to provide your organization with a higher level of security on multiple fronts.

In developing an information governance policy that incorporates security, a set of guidelines that are geared specifically towards your organization should be implemented. The first step would be to identify what information each department needs and what information departments or outside organizations need in order to communicate efficiently. Passwords, encryption, and access to documents would then be geared toward meeting the needs of specific departments or functions. In addition, only the information necessary to perform the function would be accessible, thereby enforcing a need-to-know policy and curbing the potential for unauthorized release of information.

At the most basic level, technology can be utilized for computer logins. These could be used for specific workstations, company e-mails, company devices, or anything else related to a company's computer system. Logins provide a virtually cost-free method to ensure only authorized users access an organization's computer, while at the same time recording electronically the identity, time, and location of someone who has logged on and/or off the system.

Another security basic of information governance is the control of physical access to buildings or specific areas within. Electronic cipher pads can require the swipe of an employee "smart card" or the entering of an individualized code number. Should an employee lose a card, this code number prevents the finder of the card from being able to gain unauthorized access to the facility. And just like the use of logins, this smart technology can record the comings and goings of employees, ensuring compliance with authorized access to specific locations. There are many forms of physical security. The needs of you organization should dictate what is implemented, but physically securing your data and your locations is a valuable piece of any information governance framework.[7]

There are also many more advanced versions of technology to control physical access through the use of biometrics. Biometrics are security systems designed to authenticate and grant access to individuals through verification that scans an employee's physical characteristic (face, eyes, palms, fingerprints, etc.). Biometrics can safely grant or deny access to individuals to areas that could contain information of high value, such as employee personal information, financial data, and network diagrams/topology.[8] Another hardware example is ID cards. ID cards work similarly to biometrics in that they grant access to areas of an organization. In addition, they also serve as a physical medium for authenticating an employee's identity to another person, such as a security guard.

Retina scanners, finger print scanners, body scanners, and speech recognition are just a few of the more advanced pieces of equipment that are available. Depending upon the level of security an organization requires, these types of devices could provide the heightened security needed.

As a part of their information governance planning, organizations need to decide what must be protected and how to control the flow of information and operational processes. Depending upon the type of information being utilized, many companies opt for encryption. Essentially, encryption takes plain text and converts it into code that hides the actual text. This is accomplished via a software program that is designed for this specific use. Users must then enter a password in order to access the encrypted document in a readable format.

Financial institutions in particular require a higher level of security than many companies because they control vast amounts of sensitive information, including social security numbers, dates of birth, and account numbers. Financial institutions are responsible for maintaining the security of their clients' funds as well as their PII. Additionally, most financial institutions are federally regulated, which requires them to adhere to legislation and industry controls. Because every function performed by a financial institution inevitably deals with sensitive personal information, financial institutions will often utilize encryption to protect the security of this information.

Technology can also assist with network security when backed by knowledgeable IT personnel who monitor the business network and consistently check for vulnerabilities in the organization's system. Through the use of technology, companies can store data and maintain a log of network activities related to the stored data. This allows professionals to monitor whether the information is safe or if and when it may have been compromised.

## STORAGE

The entire contents of a library may now be carried on a flash drive. Servers, databases, and file systems have made the storage and subsequent access of information much easier. Whereas it once could have taken hours to find a specific piece of information, such data can now be located in mere seconds, all thanks to advances in technology.

Technology makes things much easier for businesses when it comes to keeping and recording information. Instead of companies storing files in a large room full of cabinets, in some cases they can keep all their information on a single server/computer. Of course, storing all of your important information on just one computer is not recommended, because the failure of that one machine could mean the loss the data within. For purposes of information governance, we want not only to ensure that information can be accessed by all who need it but also to make sure that the information is stored safely and securely.

For a smaller company, a good solution for such vulnerabilities might be to have multiple computers with minimal information on each, so that it is necessary for employees to connect with one another in order to share information. This not only partitions information, which can help avoid loss or damage to all data, but also provides built in accountability. No one employee is able to take any information in an unauthorized manner without obtaining the assistance of a second employee. Based on the concept of need-to-know, a lone employee would likely not be able access information to which they are not privileged.

Risk can be further mitigated by limiting access of each computer to only the data storage relevant to that employee's responsibilities. Someone from another department may have no need to view that information. Rules such as this can limit accidents and malicious behavior. Further, for the best information governance of data storage, employees should be taught and regularly reminded always to keep their computers locked by password when not in use. This simple act will prevent others from walking up to a computer and obtaining unauthorized access to whatever data may be within. Ensuring that an employee assigned to a specific work station is responsible for the computer in that station will not only reduce vulnerability to prying eyes but will also better enable information governance personnel to determine where access was obtained should an unauthorized access take place.

Obviously, no one solution is perfect for protecting all stored information. Though the Internet is a potential limitless vault for storing information, the possibility of loss is always present. However, there are a number of steps that can be taken toward the goal of making it extremely difficult for hackers or other threats to reach classified information.

Technology has not only improved the capacity of data storage but also its cost. As more information has been stored electronically, the related costs have gone down.

Compare the difference between paying to store one terabyte of document information at the rate of about $100 per month versus printing out this information, storing the documents in hundreds of filing cabinets, and then paying for office space every month to store these cabinets. This cost savings alone has allowed businesses to grow. In turn, businesses can create more information in an effort to be more productive.

Information governance for data storage is implemented through the use of networks via the Internet. The implementation of solid information governance policies in this arena of technology can be further achieved by using an integrated network system that allows an organization to store data in different locations. By doing so, if one server is compromised by an intrusion or other damage, any other possible collateral damage is prevented.

## VPN

Virtual Private Networks (VPN) can be used to securely transmit information via long distance networks or IP addresses. This crucial tool allows companies to access files and information whether overseas on business trips or working at home. Data is often at its most vulnerable while moving from one machine to another. A VPN allows for safe and secure transmission of information and has the further benefit of being able to identify who accessed what and when, increasing accountability.

# Concerns Brought About by Technology

While many businesses rely on this technology to keep their information organized and safe, it is important to understand that even computer systems operating under the guidelines of information governance plans are not going to be perfect. The 2013 Target stores loss of customer credit card data is a prime example of how—despite the security measures in place—technology will always provide opportunities for criminals to find or create gaps in the system. The ease that technology brings to information governance also comes with many downsides.

Paying close attention and setting up management processes around your use of technology and data are important, not just from a security standpoint but from an effectiveness standpoint. Information must be governed to keep up with challenges on both the security side and the profitability side. You don't run your business to be secure; you run it to be profitable. In order to be profitable you need to be secure. It is all about balance.

Some of the issues that come from the increase in data and the speed of technology are discussed below. By no means is this an all-inclusive list. It is ever changing. Your policies and procedures need to be updated constantly, as should your understanding of technology.

## ALTERATION

Because physical data records are by their very nature physical, it is difficult for them to be accidentally or purposefully altered. However, in today's era of business records being predominantly electronic, records can easily be changed to reflect information other than what was originally recorded. Think of the possible results if someone altered bank records or—even worse—health records. This is a major reason why limiting access is so vital. You have heard the phrase "good fences make good neighbors." The same applies to employees. Give your people what they need, but do not give them more than they need.

## BALANCE

While we certainly consider technology to be a good thing, it is important to remember to maintain a balance when implementing technical solutions. After all, the main business of business is profit. Each decision to implement a greater measure of security needs to be evaluated for appropriateness and cost benefit. Likewise, the level of security for different slices of data needs to be analyzed. Would the unauthorized disclosure of certain information really result in a significant consequence?[8] Complicated steps and passwords can be a hindrance on a simple transaction, which might encourage employees to find ways to circumvent the systems if getting the needed result is too difficult or time consuming. A balance is needed between the protection of information and productivity within a business environment.[9]

## CYBERCRIME

Advances in technology have opened up a new area of crime that did not previously exist. The criminals of today have grown up in an era where technology was always second nature to them, and they are comfortable to operating in this world. It is only natural that those who are predisposed to break the law will be more inclined to engage in what they know. Hence, we now have the age of the electronic theft of money.

Fortunately, law enforcement agencies use technology to catch criminals that commit cybercrimes, much of which the general public understands. A seventeen-year-old computer hacker allegedly committed the aforementioned Target store intrusion. Bank account information was stolen from millions of people, resulting in over one billion dollars in losses, but the criminal was caught far away in Russia. Because of the Internet, it has never been easier to leave a "paper trail," even if doing so is entirely unintentional.

Every piece of electronic business a person conducts will leave behind a digital footprint. Today's law enforcement on the local, state, and federal levels are trained to track and apprehend cybercriminals. Further facilitating a successful resolution to these cybercases is the fact that much of the evidence in the technical world is very difficult to destroy. An intrusion to a computer service will leave server logs documenting the IP address of who committed the crime. If the criminal was smart enough to use a hop point (using some else's IP address without consent), this hop point can be tracked back to the original IP. When you delete something from your computer, it is never really gone. You have only given your computer an instruction to pretend the information is no longer there and permission to write over that space with new data. But just as if it was electronic Whiteout, the new data can often be lifted to reveal what is left underneath. In addition, the hard drive itself is difficult to destroy. Even when someone attempts to do so, skilled forensic examiners can still retrieve some data from the device.

## Conclusion

The introduction of commonly used technology to information governance has made the implementation of these policies both extremely complex and incredibly simple. Technology can be employed in many ways to secure information, and in the Information Age this is more important than it has ever been before. Because of this, every time the next big thing in technology released, which is happening faster and faster, many organizations will seek to employee these systems in an effort to keep their information as secure as possible.

It is important to remember that no matter how promising the technology, nothing is 100 percent foolproof. Despite technological advances, with enough persistence eventually any skilled hacker will be able to access a chosen system. And just as technology is advancing to keep information safe, the criminal cyberelement is always developing more tools in an effort to defeat these systems.

The best solution when using technology as a defense to protect information is to employ multiple levels. Various data security measures, like solid firewalls, are important to your information governance plan. So are employing good technology safety measures, such as strong passwords to prevent unauthorized access. And just as important is constant education about continually evolving threats. With all the technology that is out there to defend our information, our worst enemy can be a leak of information by just one person who can potentially compromise an entire system—and possibly do so without ever even knowing it.

In a technological world that is slowly becoming more of a target for online threats, data attacks, and the loss of files and information, technology also has to be part of the solution. Information must be properly governed and protected, for it is not a question of if but when an online data attack will happen.

# References

1. "Information Governance," last updated November 2013, accessed December 2013. http://searchcompliance.echtarget.com/definition/information-governance/.
2. Guile, I. (2014, January 18). A soon to be popular breach. Retrieved from University of Advancing Technology Internet.
3. "Information governance."
4. "Massive Target Data Breach Strategy 'new to eCrime': Security Report," January 16, 2014, accessed December 2013. http://investigations.nbcnews.com/_news/2014/01/16/22330454-massive-target-data-breach-strategy-new-to-ecrime-security-report/.
5. Debra Logan, "What is Information Governance? And Why is It So Hard?" *The Gartner Blog Network*, January 11, 2010, accessed December 2013. http://blogs.gartner.com/debra_logan/2010/01/11/what-is-information-governance-and-why-is-it-so-hard/.
6. Rudy Moliere, Leigh Isaacs, and Samantha Lofton, "Predictive Coding for Information Governance," in *Emerging Trends in Law Firm Information Governance* (Iron Mountain Inc., 2013), p. 6, accessed December 2013. http://www.greenheartllc.com/images/LFIGS2013Emerging_Trends_in_Information_Governance_2013.pdf.
7. Logan, "What is Information Governance?"
8. David Cowan, "Comment: Too Much Security May Affect Business Practices," June 27, 2012, accessed December 2013. http://www.infosecurity-magazine.com/view/26550/comment-too-much-security-may-affect-business-processes/.
9. Ibid.

# Chapter 8

# Balancing Information Governance and Your Company's Mission

To this point, we have spent quite a bit of time exploring the various aspects of information governance and the clear benefits a solid plan can bring to an organization. However, the question remains whether an information governance plan will be compatible with your organization's current structure. How difficult will it be? How much will it positively or adversely impact the bottom-line?

While these questions might seem to imply that information governance is being forced upon a business, the fact remains that some business models were established without ever taking information governance into account and are therefore not designed in a manner that would easily permit the introduction of internal checks and balances, policies, and procedures regarding your IT systems and data.

None of this is to suggest that you should re-create your business model from the ground up to incorporate information governance, although doing so can pay dividends in corporate security. The phrasing of the question seems to suggest that information governance and a profitable business are in some ways mutually exclusive. That is to say, any gain to one comes at the expense of the other. To move toward adopting information governance would be to move away from profitability.

It is understandable that it may be difficult to move away from this line of thinking while you are metaphorically trying to fit the square information governance peg into a round business model hole. After all, the corporate environment is in the business of being profitable. The very ecosystem of a successful corporation seems to ensure that any procedures, checks and balances, or behaviors acting in contradiction to that goal are identified and neutralized. If information governance is one of those things that are inhibiting profitability, then surely it will be discounted.

The question of how a business should draw the line between having information governance policies protect their important data while not inhibiting the ability to conduct business is difficult to answer. Information governance can be a matter of two extremes: either being protected or not protected. Will giving too many resources to the former inhibit the ability for a company as a whole to function? After all, how much protection is too much? It is definitely not an easy question to answer, and the issues of increased efficiency, improved productivity, and fewer losses need to be evaluated.

## Policies

All businesses should have some form of plan or system in which information is handled or gathered. Systems such as the Generally Accepted Privacy Principles are the mainstay in most businesses today.[1] Having a system to follow will limit the possibility of mishandled information while streamlining in-business dealings to be faster and more efficient. In addition, the cost to manage the system should not cut into the business's profit too much. Exactly how much should be decided by the business itself as a part of an overall strategic plan.

Businesses can remain fairly secure by having plans that confine their data to business quarters and a limited number of employees, consistently managing employee regulations, and adhering to a pre-determined system of information handling. Following these basic practices will streamline business affairs without compromising the security of private data. If at any point privacy policies begin to impede too much on efficiency, then the business should re-work its plans. An ideal plan actually improves efficiency. The information governance committee should have improving business processes as a task. Policies should be measured and systematically evaluated.

To avoid issues, a business should carefully create company policies and utilize current technologies to find that fine line between security and profitability. Developing such plans is not a one-time event. Rather, it should remain an ongoing process. Part of the company plan should be to make full use of employee resources, making sure employees who handle sensitive information are properly educated on the requirements of their jobs and that they have read and understand the company policies. A slight lapse by one employee can cause an error that is catastrophic to the company.

In addition to education, companies need to dedicate a percentage of their financial resources to keeping technology up to date in order to maintain the protection of company information (and to constantly improve efficiency). Companies with strong protections are less likely to become victims. Of course, there will always be risks and threats, but the goal of information governance is to conduct business while mitigating risks. Companies need to work constantly to maintain the balance between profitability and security. Deciding just how much risk an organization is willing to assume must be covered in the company's information governance plan.

## STRENGTHS AND WEAKNESSES

In assessing the introduction of information governance policies versus maintaining the current operations of an organization, sometimes the only thing that stands in the way of progress is how the organization chooses to look at the proposed changes. Are they strengths or weaknesses? In doing this, we depart from a paradigm of seeking forcibly to insert information governance policies upon a company, choosing instead to begin by accounting for both the risks and benefits of all things information governance. By doing so, we can highlight newly available solutions to old issues.

Possible points of contention seen when forcing information governance into an existing corporate structure can be categorized into positive and negative gains. Negatives that arise due to an incompatibility of the old corporate structure and the inclusion of information governance can be viewed as an opportunity for improvement. Assume for example that an organization learns in advance that the government or law enforcement could subpoena private customer information. If a company were to offer private communication services. a conflict of interests would exist, as the power of subpoena jeopardizes this privacy. If the company were aware of such possibilities in the beginning stages of corporate development, alternatives could be considered that might not be feasible in cases where information governance is later added to an established environment.

In regards to the problem of private information being obtained via subpoena, policies could be modified to decide how user information could alternatively be stored. Restrictions could be implemented that prohibits the organization from accessing a client's private information without the client's password. In this way, both corporate and user interests are shielded in a manner that ensures compliance with regulations and cooperation with law enforcement. In addition, the company's marketing can use this feature an additional enhancement in attracting more clients. Often, it is all a matter of how companies choose to look at the possibilities and act upon them.

## BALANCE

Balance is a common theme within information governance, as it is in many facets of running a business. Think of balancing the expense of retooling a factory with the cost savings it would allow. Having secure procedures and policies that balance with an organization's processes that require meticulous planning and implementation is much the same. The need for balance between these two is important, because having too much or too little of one can spell misfortune for businesses.

Having very limited information governance policies could leave a business unprotected and data vulnerable, whereas implementing too many such policies could affect the way a business functions, thereby curtailing profits. However, because each business has different procedures, goals, culture, management hierarchy, etc., it would be impractical to create a one size fits all for every company to follow.

For example, a small business such as a bookstore will have vastly different needs than a million-dollar corporation in terms of employees, systems, and information. Therefore, an effective start to creating a balance for security and business needs is to identify and analyze the most critical areas of the organization. A good place to begin would be anything that holds valuable information such as databases, servers, and workstations. The next step would be to determine the risks that could affect those services, such as natural disasters, malicious software, physical theft, and other threats. Once the important areas and risks associated with them are identified, businesses must adopt measures to detect, deter, and mitigate these risks.

This may sound like a relatively simple and straightforward process, but as stated above the difficulty lies in creating a balance between information governance and business operations. The solution at times can be to implement very few policies—or sometimes not to implement any policies at all, depending on the risk. If, for example, one of the biggest risks to an organization is an employee stealing office supplies, the best solution would be to install a security camera or have employee training that show the effects and consequences of stealing office supplies. A needless and overly burdensome solution would be to implement an abundance of costly information governance policies, such as hiring security guards to watch the employees. The balance addresses the basic problems and leaves out controls that are not actually needed the majority of the time.

## Varying Approaches

While there is no reason to deny the point that the goal of all companies is to make a profit, these goals can be quite different from one company to another based upon the business they are in. Because of these differences, every decision made for the various business aspects is going to vary from one company to the next. Their approaches to information governance are no exception.

The type of business determines where the line is drawn regarding the level at which information needs to be protected. For a financial institution, the line may be drawn where customer information ends and their personal banking information begins. The same may be said of medical institutions where personal information is deemed to be sensitive. The point, of course, is that once sensitive information—personal, financial, medical, or anything of the sort—is involved, the line must be drawn in the interest of protection through the implementation of information governance.

Another way of examining the issue of when information governance is needed is to focus not on how a business makes money but instead look at how a business attracts and retains its customers. For instance, financial institutions have always attracted customers by assuring them that their money was safe. As we have moved beyond the days of cash and are now more focused on accounts and credits, the collateral of a financial institution now includes their clients' personal information and bank account numbers as well as the balances in their respective accounts. The same rules now apply for medical institutions and private businesses. While the approaches may vary, all businesses need to establish certain levels of security procedures to ensure the information they collect remains secured. A security breach or a leak would be disastrous for any business regardless of their power or status. As was the case for the 2013 data breach at Target, although the breach did not destroy the company it did adversely impact its reputation and financial performance.

## WEIGHING THE BENEFITS

By working together with your company's IT department or equivalent experts on your current set-up for data management, a better understanding can be gained of where the company stands regarding information governance and, more importantly, how much your company needs to further achieve. All of this is considered against the background of the company's earning capacity.

A good rule of thumb when considering the implementation of information governance policies is that the more value your company places on something, the more likely it is that someone else wants to have it and is willing to break the law to get it. Just like money, information has to be stored and secured somewhere. And the more information you have the more of a valuable target your company will become. Hence the need to invest some of the organization's profits into dependable security measures.

Generally, those in charge of the organization will already understand this and be willing to listen to viable solutions. What is often not understood is that expensive security measures might actually be more than needed or not worth the cost for the results they produce. Employing such extreme measures ends up negatively affecting the company by having security that is too restrictive. The business might become frustrated under the weight of security, especially if the policies forbid new technologies, applications, or devices that the company wants to adopt. Rules and policies can expand and become more restrictive until they are too rigid to allow the company to compete and innovate.[2] The reward of safer and smoother information governance should always be balanced against the risk of upsetting your workers and limiting your company's growth and efficiency.

## Team Effort

Corporate structures consist of compartmentalized sections focused on groups of goals with similar responsibilities. Although a part of the same organizational, these compartments are a mix of forces involving rivalry and competition over allocated resources such as budgetary funds and symbiotic dependencies. Software programmers could not work on nonexistent blueprints that were not produced by the engineers who were not made aware of the needs and expectations of the project until direction was provided by management.

All of this is understood to be a risk to workflow productivity in a corporate environment, and these functions of communication and information transfer are taken into account as the corporation is established and continues to grow. Such risks are known and accommodated by allowing amendments to policy as new situations arise. Unfortunately, this can also lead to contradicting statements in policies from differing sections of the corporation, as sections are updated without having a full understanding of the greater vision or favoritism is displayed toward some departments over others. In time, this may serve to undermine the founding ideals of the company.

It is also possible that old policies where created in a manner that addressed issues as they existed in an earlier time. Those policies may have once been satisfactory but perhaps did not take into account advances in technology, the increase in the amount of data, or the speed with which it can be transmitted. However, efforts to update antiquated policies could be met with contention by some, based on fears of disrupting those policies that are already in place. For some the older policies assure the inner-operability of the corporation.

A key characteristic of any successful information governance initiative is the establishment of an enterprise-wide approach that clearly sets out roles and responsibilities, emphasizing that everyone has a part to play in enabling successful IT outcomes.[3] Implementation of effective information governance depends on everyone having adequate and appropriate skills to fulfil their specific role. In most organizations, investors and controllers will have a good understanding of governance principles but usually have a poor understanding of how to apply these principles in the world of IT. Likewise, although IT specialists understand IT, they may have a poor appreciation of governance and control principles.[4]

## Decision Makers

Whoever is in the appropriate decision-making role in the company may not be fully equipped to make the best decisions when it comes to working out an approach to information governance. By its nature, information governance involves the ever-evolving technology employed by a company to keep its data stored, organized, and safe. Depending upon the type of corporation, those in leadership positions are not always the foremost experts in their own technology. After all, this is why companies employee IT personnel. Often, those in charge will consult tech-savvy individuals from their IT department to develop solid plans for the company's information governance systems. Alternatively, there are many traps into which higher-ups can fall into by making uninformed decisions, the consequences of which could include losing large amounts of the company's information and money.

Likewise, decision makers need to ensure that the IT is managed appropriately, because in a technological world the key to disrupting business is to disrupt IT. Organizations should strive to have trusted managers to oversee sensitive data, regulate the sharing and safety of data, and ensure efficient operation for everyone's benefit. Doing so allows employees to access the information they need to conduct their work quickly and efficiently.

An effective information governance program is best developed and driven by a committee with a senior leader at the helm who is not in charge of IT. Having someone leading the way with a qualified team but without pre-conceived notions and alliances is your best bet to developing the balance you need.

# Factors to Consider

## GUIDELINES

In establishing information governance polices for an organization, it is important to have established guidelines for all departments or sectors of a business. A business needs to implement proper policies that appropriately address how the information in a business is both stored and used by those within the organization.

The first step in establishing guidelines would be to identify what type of information each department needs. Businesses can achieve efficient information governance by outlining specific demands for the information the company holds. In creating proper policies, an understanding of and compliance with applicable laws is crucial. Once the law is understood, a company can tailor a policy that is within the standards of the law but is most effective for their type of business. Efficiency with information governance will help mitigate risks with cost. A company should not store data that it does not need to conduct its business. Excess data can cause unneeded problems and increase cost for data storage.

The next step in the guidelines process is to determine what departments and outside organizations require in order to communicate efficiently. Passwords, encryption, and access to documents would then be established for that department or function. In addition, only the information necessary to perform the function would be accessible. For example, a transaction at a retail store does not require a social security number, but a human resources department does.

## SOCIAL MEDIA

In today's society, online information is one area where businesses can potentially be very vulnerable. Social media websites like Facebook and Twitter can be great ways to spread promotions and new products your company has to offer. However, these same websites can also spread very sensitive data via posts by current or former employees.

It's important for businesses to give their employees guidelines on how to represent themselves and their company online, especially as it pertains to their personal social media pages. These rules should be made part of the company's information governance polices, with specific language addressing what current or former employees may say regarding the company and its services, as well as the potential civil ramifications for breaching the policy.

For example, if a former employee posts information on one of the social media websites that details confidential corporate information, such as formulas or how products are made, the release of this information can be devastating to the company. If the information governance polices does not contain specific language specifying limitations, the offending party can defend themselves against liability by pointing out that nothing in the company's regulations prohibited such actions.

Even in cases where it is not necessarily intentional, employees who post information on corporate developments can be equally harmful to the company. By posting information boasting about the company's future success, employees may be tipping off the competition or giving the competitors ideas they might not have even considered. Therefore, information governance policies need to cover employee behaviors both on and off duty; behaviors which can potentially impact the organization.

It is important to note that information governance policies that address employee conduct have to be carefully considered before being implemented. As an employer, you want your employees to be happy and have some sense of freedom. Forcing employees to delete their entire social media accounts before being hired or while working for a company will generally create a sense of dissatisfaction, especially today when many people see social media websites as a significant part of their social life.

To the contrary, information governance policies can actually encourage employees to share their love for their work and their employer via social media websites. Rather than language that discourages social media use, policies can be drafted encouraging persons to engage in the behavior they want but cautioning against certain dangers. Likewise, these same policies can provide examples of permissible postings on social media, so that employees have a clearer understanding of what to do and what not to do. By not discouraging the use of social media yet limiting the potential exposure to threats, companies may very well reap the benefit of further publicity through the efforts of their employees. The best way to implement information governance policies regarding social media is to have a balance between freedom and restrictions. It is important to protect your company's valued information, just as it is also important to share with the world the positive things that your company is achieving. At the end of the day, revenue can be generated by companies, without revealing vital information, by advertising themselves in the proper professional manner through the social media posts of employees.

Companies should also have established policies covering what is the permissible use of social media during office hours. The personal use of social media during work hours can result in a significant loss of productivity. It is estimated that 50% of all corporate bandwidth is being used by employees to view social media, check e-mail, and surf the web. While companies can encourage some downtime for employees to recoup and recharge, the Internet can equally prove to be a distraction from the mission. Good information governance policies will not only outline what can be posted but also permissible times to use social media during work hours, such as on approved breaks and during lunch.

## Costs

Some aspects of information governance can be expensive. Security measures, system monitoring, and training are all time consuming and come with a cost. It may be easy to look at the expenditure of both time and profits and decide it is not worth the efforts or expense. However, while there are expenses associated with information governance, it is potentially more expensive to defend against lawsuit for not sufficiently protecting the integrity of sensitive information or to provide mitigation to those who have been victimized by a breach. In many ways, information governance is like insurance. You hope never to use it, but you are certainly glad to have it when needed.

This does not mean, however, that every dollar made should be invested toward the protection of that dollar. There is a point where protecting your assets may hamper your company's abilities to acquire those assets in the first place. This is where the line must be drawn. If a company is spending more on protecting information than the information is worth, then this line has been crossed. It may be difficult to determine exactly how much employee or customer information is worth in monetary value, but once the risk for leaking any of it is small enough, pouring more time and resources into this effort becomes a diminishing return. While there is something to be said for the phrase "better safe than sorry," the expression "a penny saved is a penny earned" also has merit.

## Profits

In most businesses, money is what decides success. It is the lifeblood of business operations and structure. When we think of information governance as protecting sensitive information, indirectly it is also about protecting the company's profits.

Like the earlier referenced business balance, the same issues have to be considered for information governance when it comes to the profits. Information that leaks into the wrong hands will likely result in major financial consequences—in other words, a loss of profits. However, an overabundance of safeguarding could be detrimental to an organization's flow of business, leading in turn to further loss of profits. Likewise, information that is restrained too securely in business operations can hinder operational functionality, thereby losing money in the process.

All this needs to be kept in mind while generating a profit. Each time a decision to implement a greater measure of security in the name of information governance is considered, the company decision makers need to take into account the type of information they are protecting and whether the possible loss outweighs the cost of protection. Can an informational asset be compromised without major consequence? Complicated steps and passwords can be a hindrance on a simple transaction. In the interest of maintaining a healthy profit margin, a balance is needed between the protection of information and productivity within a business environment.[5]

## COMMUNICATIONS

When developing an information governance strategy, a business needs to determine how it conducts both its internal and external communications. These communication lines will inevitably be affected by any additions of information governance policies.

Having information governance plans is one thing, but effectively communicating them to your employees and customers is another. Changes or brand new implementations need to be communicated properly to your employees to ensure the methods are being utilized in the proper manner. Likewise, by communicating these changes or implementations to an organization's customers, the business can effectively gain consumer confidence, which can possibly translate into increased revenue.

Another necessity is to understand how information governance policies could negatively impact the flow and level of communication. New or more complicated procedures can delay request from both employee and outside customers. Response times can also be slowed. It may be that before policies were implemented everyone in that company had access to certain information, but now procedures create checks and balances in releasing information. Companies must communicated to their employees how best to minimize any new delays that might have developed, while also communicating to customers how these potential delays are in their best interest because they ensure information security.

To help in these situations, a business should implement some type of easily accessible, cross-functional team that caters to the company. A cross-functional team would be able to bridge a gap between the various parties responsible for new information governance policies, teams making requests, and those who handle information.[3] Using a team as opposed to a single contact allows multiple eyes to create checks and balance for good governance. It also keeps the lines of communication open to reduce delays.

## CULTURE

Whenever changes are contemplated, an organization must be aware of the corporate culture that exists and how it may be impacted by any potential changes. The acceptance of change will vary from business to business. Because many people are reluctant to embrace change, organizations need to be aware of any potential impact that the change may have on their employees (which can negatively affect productivity) as well as the impact that change can have on clientele (which can affect customer loyalty).

One of the best ways to help merge information governance into a corporate culture is for the leaders of the change to embrace awareness. Having employees and customers aware of policy changes coming well in advance allows time for both parties to adjust to the new way of working.[6] A staggered approach to implementing policies also gives employees and customers time to figure out how to work optimally within these new policies. This allows minimal disruption to a business's culture and allows it to continue operating at a (mostly) normal level. This is critical to the company's ability to conduct itself in a proper manner.

Significant benefits can be gained for the organization by tailoring the policies wherever possible to match the existing businesses culture. Allow sufficient time for various aspects of the new information governance policies to be put into effect gradually, rather than a wholesale implementation of new rules overnight.[7] Allowing time for adjustment to a few new policies alongside normal operations will lessen the apprehension of those who—regardless of the benefits—do not embrace change. It is ultimately not what policies are implemented but how and when they are implemented that can affect a business. While information governance is important to the functionality of a company, it also needs to make allowanced for a user-friendly environment for the clients. It is important that a company's clientele can still be provided with the necessary products and services to which they are accustomed.

## CIA

Information governance includes the concept of CIA: confidentiality, integrity, and availability.[8] The absence of any of these three concepts undermines the proper practice of information governance policies.

Confidentiality is the prevention of information disclosure to unauthorized individuals or systems. If information governance policies did not adequately maintain the confidentiality of research and development files, and these files were to be accessed by a rival company, the loss of confidential information would have a negative affect on the company.

Integrity ensures that the information has not been altered and is recorded and stored accurately. Easily gaining access to information is not of any value if the information in question is not what it should have been. In the interest of saving money on the cost of storage, a company would never consider randomly deleting sections of documents. Ensuring information integrity is crucial to supporting information governance.

Availability is the ability to access information when it is needed. If an organizational leader needs information for a shareholders meeting, but cannot access the files, the availability of this information is too low and will undoubtedly have a negative impact on the perception by the shareholders. If the availability of information is so low that the people who need it cannot access it, the information cannot properly serve its purpose. Information, no matter how valuable, is essentially worthless if it cannot be used to carry out tasks for which it is needed.

All three aspects of CIA must work together to achieve the necessary balance for information governance to function in the sought-after fashion. Too much or too little of any of these attributes will cause information governance to fail. Businesses should therefore apply these concepts on a case-by-case basis. Within the corporate structure, various documents may call for various levels of security. Research and development may be guarded more securely than lesser administrative functions like plans for company fire drills. Elements of CIA will need to be applied to all aspects of information, but it is up to the organization's leaders to decide upon where and how much.

## SECURITY

How does a business balance making money with mitigating risk to their data or information? Measures that can be set in place to help a company run smoothly in terms of making money while also accomplishing the mission of information security. Before determining what information governance policies to undertake, we first have to determine exactly what needs to be secured. Like reading a map, once we figure out where we want to go, we can then figure out how best to get there.

Every company—from the smallest operation to the large corporation—will have a certain amount of PII. Employee dates of birth, social security numbers, and bank account numbers for payroll deposits are all maintained by the company, and the company must be responsible for securing this information.

Next is the concern for the security of customer information. A company might have bank account information for their purchasers and suppliers. Those doing business with the public can accumulate a significant amount of credit card numbers. Those in the business of issuing credit cards will have the personal information of potentially millions of customers.

From a business standpoint, information governance plays a vital role in keeping both information and a company's reputation secure. However, security all comes down to finding that delicate balance. While protecting the company's reputation, if things become protected to the point that security is too difficult to manage, security can actually work against the information governance plan.

Overly complicated passwords can become a nuisance to input every time if it is too demanding for the employee to remember. When password requirements become too complicated, employees will opt to write them down so that they do not forget. The intent behind a complex password is noble but can undermine the effort by allowing prying eyes to obtain the written password. Companies should require passwords difficult enough to deter hackers but not so complex as to discourage use by their employees.

Also, it is also an excellent idea to require passwords to be changed at regular intervals, usually anywhere from three to six months. Regardless of security measures that are in place, it is inevitable that an employee will in some manner lose, forget, or share their password, which compromises security integrity. By mandating regular password changes and not permitting recently used passwords to be recycled into use again, the threat of hack or other breaches of password security can be greatly diminished.

Clearance level access is a security method used in organizations that have highly classified information that must be kept secret. Various employees will possess various levels of clearance in order to obtain data secured at different levels. Overclassifying information unnecessarily or not compartmentalizing out unclassified information from a classified document will limit the availability of the data for those who might need to work with this information.

Most hackers do not want to spend an enormous amount of time trying to get into a company's system. Most hackers prefer the easy steal. By incorporating a few basics into a company's network security plan, many of the threats of unauthorized intrusion to a network can be eliminated. Sensitive data on a company network should have levels of security to minimize the threat of being hacked, but there are basic and balanced steps a company can take to limit this threat without applying overly complicated methodologies.

The first step would be to limit who has access to the network. Of course, an organization wants its IT people to be able to access the network, but there may be others in the company who have a need as well. Determining who has a need and who does not can limit the accidental or purposeful exposure of the company's network security.

Second, from what locations can the network be accessed? Again, you probably want your IT personnel to be able to access the network any time of the day from anywhere in order to immediately address problems that might occur. But do other personnel have the same needs? Should employees be able to work from home on their personal computer, when the company does not know how secure that computer may be before it accesses the corporate system? Malware on the home computer can be spread to the work computer. Requiring employees to take home a work laptop that is securely maintained solves the problem of working from home without threatening network security.

Likewise, what about the times when the network can be accessed? IT may have a reason to be on the network day and night, but the average employee probably does not. By limiting network access to business hours or when a laptop has been checked out to work from home or while away on business, those monitoring information governance security will be able to see who is accessing the system at odd hours. Those not authorized to do so may be accessing the system for nefarious reasons that can then be prevented.

Training is one of the greatest and most cost-effective ways to ensure an organization's level of information security. If training is conducted at regular intervals and with repetition of subject, employees are likely to grasp the importance of the security standards and better adhere to the policies.

The use of technology to help keep data secure is forever changing. At times it can be difficult for everyone within the organization to comprehend. These difficulties could cause annoyance, which can then translate into a lack of concern on the part of some employees. However, with an investment of a minimal amount of time, employees can receive refresher training to ensure they are comfortable with their roles in securing information.

Likewise, most attacks such as cold calling for social engineering and e-mail scams that contain malware are successful against persons who are least familiar with proper information governance. Knowledgeable employees can stop most basic attacks themselves, as well as inform IT personnel so that the rest of the company can be made aware of the attempted attacks. The minimal downtime from work to provide regular employee training will more than pay for itself in the avoidance of corrupted networks and monetary expenses to repair the damage of compromised information.

Companies walk a fine line in trying to decide how much security is needed for their organization in order to balance the needs of business verses the needs of information safety. Companies need to decide what is important, and each department needs to gauge importance. An all-in-one policy can hinder certain profit areas. Each security measure needs to be company and department specific, and to provide a clear understanding employees about information that is readily accessible and data that needs to be more securely protected.

## NEED-TO-KNOW

In order to limit sensitive data from seeping outside the boundaries of where it should be confined, businesses should take steps to permit data to be accessed only by those who require access for specified purposes. This aspect of information security can be accomplished in several manners.

One of the more prominent ways to limit corporate information to those who have a need to know is though the use of in-house software. By utilizing programs that are not necessarily off the shelf but rather designed specifically for a particular company's business needs, it makes it much more difficult for employees to abscond with information if they do not have the software necessary to read the information. This allows a business much greater control over its private data.

The idea of business specific software can be taken even further by having different software programs for different branches of a company's operation. This enables the company to further limit their data and other sensitive information to only those who have access to these particular programs. Lower-level employees will only have limited access, and access will increase as employees have more specific functions or hold higher positions within the organization.

Additionally, by maintaining this software and the accompanying data in in-business databases separated from the open web, businesses do not have to rely on firewalls and other networking security to ensure their information is not compromised through computer intrusion. This allows for clean, efficient data management without hindrance or data flow impediments. In the end, this mean the primary locus for information slippage is the employees themselves.

It is important for only those employees that need to use certain information to be the ones with access to that information. A company should have policies that allow employees to do their jobs and ensures appropriate access to information while also requiring employees to be accountable for their actions. If an employee is dealing with crucial information, they need to know how to handle it appropriately.[9]

## MITIGATION OF RISKS

In order to find the balance between information governance and a company's ability to conduct business, there needs to be a balance of protective measures within the company and measures that mitigate potential risks. The company must decide how much risk they can afford in the event of lost or misused data and information without hamstringing operations to the point that clientele is discouraged from doing business and instead seeks out a competitor that operates more freely. Similarly, if a company is not secure enough, the company can be the victim of data loss, espionage by a competitor, and a variety of other events. Nevertheless, there are some basics any organization can undertake to mitigate their risks from some of the more common threats.

Mitigating the risk of employees misplacing data begins before the new employee is even hired. Thorough background checks should be undertaken to ensure that personnel are qualified for the position they are being sought to fill. Are these employees being recruited from a rival company? Do they have designs on starting their own competing business? Do they have a history of criminal offenses or arrests, especially ones involving cybercrimes and the compromise of information? Are these individuals experienced at handling sensitive information and, if so, how successful were they at performing these duties? As part of the pre-employment screening of a company's information governance plan, these questions and others should be asked before new hires are welcomed on board. In doing this, the likelihood of a purposeful data-leak by a less-than-trustworthy employee is greatly reduced.

Once hired, it is equally important for all new hires to be thoroughly briefed on the company's information governance policies. Just as efforts were expended to limit the potential for an intentional data leak, these efforts will greatly reduce the likelihood of an accidental leak. Furthermore, consideration should be given occasionally to administering employee testing to monitor their knowledge of and consistency in following the company's information governance rules.

## CLOSING THOUGHTS

The primary goal of any business is making money. However, a business in the pursuit of profit should not do so by being careless with their most valuable data, whether it be employee information, network topologies, access credentials, financial data, or any other critical information. Instead, businesses need to balance the goal of making money with the necessity of solid information governance policies. The trick is to find the proper balance. The fine line that allows a company to protect valuable data and yet remain profitable is up to each company to determine for themselves. In today's world, the two functions can no longer be mutually exclusive.

## References

1. "Generally Accepted Privacy Principles," accessed December, 2013. http://www.aicpa.org/interestareas/informationtechnology/resources/privacy/generallyacceptedprivacyprinciples/pages/default.aspx.
2. Andreas M. Antonopoulos, "Can You Have Too Much Security?" May 31, 2011, accessed February 2014. http://www.networkworld.com/article/2177700/security/can-you-have-too-much-security-.html.
3. ISACA, *An Introduction to the Business Model for Information Security* (Rolling Meadows, Ill.: ISACA, 2009), 12. http://www.isaca.org/Knowledge-Center/BMIS/Documents/IntrotoBMIS.pdf.
4. Ibid.
5. David Cowan, "Comment: Too Much Security May Affect Business Practices," June 27, 2012, accessed December, 2013. http://www.infosecurity-magazine.com/view/26550/comment-too-much-security-may-affect-business-processes/.
6. IT governance, 2005, 25.
7. ISACA, *Introduction*, p. 13.
8. Terry Chia, "Confidentiality, Integrity, and Availability: The Three Components of the CIA Triad," *IT Security Community Blog*, August 20, 2012, accessed December, 2013. http://security.blogoverflow.com/2012/08/confidentiality-integrity-availability-the-three-components-of-the-cia-triad/.
9. Debra Logan, "What is Information Governance? And Why is It So Hard?" *The Gartner Blog Network*, January 11, 2010, accessed December, 2013. http://blogs.gartner.com/debra_logan/2010/01/11/what-is-information-governance-and-why-is-it-so-hard/.

# The Case for Information Governance from within Your Organization

Ok, so you get it. You see why and how information governance can protect and benefit your company. The question now is, how will you convince everyone else? What key attributes can be shown to encourage your business to embrace information governance policies? How can you incorporate the policies into the fabric of your organization? How do you make information governance become a part of the your company's culture?

First, an organization should be informed about information governance and how it affects the company. The business needs to have a solid set of policies outlining its information governance to specifically handle any and all any types of lawsuits that might arise. The cost of such an event could prove fatal for a business, and the business could go under without the proper information governance program and policies. Simple? Yes. But does it answer all the questions? No.

The most important information to convince a budding business about the importance of information governance is knowledge of the risks that already exist. This could be easily described as a "scare tactic" —a description that is not necessarily untrue. It was not until the authors were sitting in a meeting discussing their own sensitive information that it really occurred to us just how potentially unsecure our own business information might be. This meeting included a demonstration of how easily information can be found about anyone by conducting a small amount of research through open sources on the Internet. This information included the authors' full name, personal addresses, jobs, credit card numbers, social security numbers, and phone numbers.

It is daunting how bad information leakage can be, and it's even more worrisome that the issue is taken so lightly today, especially by companies that are most at risk for losing the personal information of their customers. Explaining these threats to your organization in a way that hits home and is personal is a great way to start the conversation. A little real-world threat goes a long way toward driving the desire to implement governance rules that will fundamentally change your business for the better.

As discussed previously, it is not all about the threats. Information governance is about preparation as well: preparing to take advantage of the benefits of improving technology, preparing your organization to adapt to change, and preparing to be more efficient and utilize technology to the fullest. Once people start to understand the benefits of clear policies and the forward-thinking information governance drives, the rest comes easy. Information governance benefits everyone.

## Negative Perceptions of Information Governance

By its very nature, information governance is a "no" program. No sharing passwords. No taking proprietary information home. No accessing areas of the network that are not imperative to your job function. No using personal e-mail on company computers. These items are all important and constitute a big part of information governance. The fact is that rules, policies, and procedures are the backbone of information governance. The threats are real, permanent, and evolving. Without those policies, a business is vulnerable. Technology today allows the bad guys to find weaknesses quickly, and without a system to combat those threats your organization will become another victim.

Putting forth the notion that you are constantly under attack is not without merit. If you are connected to the Internet, you are constantly being pinged and tested by the criminal element, whether they be a lone individual engaged in cybercrime, a competitor who is seeking to compromise your organization to a gain a business advantage, or even a hostile nation that is more interested in stealing trade secrets than paying for them. Through the use of computer systems that are constantly scanning the Internet looking for open nodes to access. These threats are always looking for the next opportunity to take advantage.

## Implementation

Start by assessing the needs of your company. It is important to understand what type of information the company has and the amount of risk associated with the information. Furthermore, it is important to understand the size and worth of the company.

This allows you to create effective information governance policies at an appropriate cost. Remember, balance is key. A small company would not need as much information governance as a large company, and it would not be economically appropriate to try and implement such.

Information governance can be compared to parenting. The rules for a two-year-old are going to be basic and simple. The rules for a ten-year-old are more defined and more complex. The rules for a seventeen-year-old are even more so. At all ages, the rules will vary by child, depending on their potential risk exposure and their history of encountering dangers. The same applies to your company. Information governance should be size and risk appropriate.

It is important for everyone in the company to be aware of the information governance processes that will be implemented. If feasible, meeting with the entire company is important in order to get everyone on the same page, but grouping people together into smaller subsets to explain more in-depth plans and changes is also appropriate. Gaining employee acceptance, understanding, and buy-in is vital to the successful implementation of these policies.

The establishment of an information governance committee is a step that will demonstrate the commitment and focus of the enterprise. This core group steers information governance for the entire company. It is tasked with developing and implementing the system, as well as keeping up with changes both internally and externally. This group, as has been indicated throughout, should include representation by IT but should not be led by IT. Rather, a senior leader in the organization who has access to those with the authority to dictate changes should lead the information governance committee.

After a committee is created, it is time to define the information governance policies and procedures. The committee needs to know how the company uses its information and how it could be compromised. Where are the vulnerabilities? What is important to the organization? How does the company change without disrupting operations? In fact, how does the company change to become even better? The policies should allow employees to do their job but not put the company at risk. The policies should not overlook employee actions, but rather should help the employee succeed at their work. Once information governance policies are in place, the company should make sure the employees are following the policies and help them if they are having troubles adapting or adhering to the changes.

Information governance policies should be a flexible system that can adapt to future changes in the company's industry. Making sure the policies are working and offering solutions to possible issues is the job of the information governance committee. The company should also establish a remediation processes to help employees follow the policies and to make recommendations to improve them. It is important to be compliant with the law and be effective in the business world, so the committee should tailor policies as they see fit to best suit the company.[1]

One point to note on implementation is the need to enforce the rules in a positive way. Looking for the means to recognize positive performance serves to motivate employees and to encourage them to maintain their attention to information governance. A few examples of simple ways to recognize employees for adhering to good information governance practices include:

- Rewarding employees that change their passwords every 60 to 90 days; and
- Offering a team reward for any efforts in securing work that resulted in zero breaches over a set period of time (think of the signs that are seen in factories that read "138 days since the last accident").

These are just a couple of ways that can make following good information governance practices fun and part of the employee's everyday work life. Additionally these policies and procedures need to be easy to follow and use. Employees will tend to steer toward the path of least resistance, as it is human nature to do so. Giving them tools along with clearly defined direction is the only sure way to gain acceptance.

Likewise, a scheduled and structured set of strategies for keeping track of the company's important information is another vital step in running a risk-reduced business. Enforcing a change in employee passwords or reminding employees not to use their company accounts for personal use are obviously good steps toward protecting the entire company from a fatal mishap. However, training and reminders can only minimize the threats to a certain degree against human error or a malicious insider. Conversely, having a system in place to make sure that employees do not (or cannot) take any critical information away from the office can be a boon in the efforts to reliably store and manage information.

Another added value is the realization that implementation of information governance can be a fresh start opportunity for wiping away practices that hinder or are detrimental to performance and growth. By changing how things are done and how a company's information is managed, the organization not only puts in place new and effective practices but is able to remove old problems. Imagine there is an old rule or habit that allows employees to access outside web-based e-mail programs on a sensitive system. Information governance not only defines how that system is used but also removes the old, risky practice and replaces it with a more streamlined, safe, and effective practice.

Not every aspect of information governance needs to be a drawn-out, expensive process requiring large amounts of company resources. Many simple steps, like the examples just listed, create a positive impact that is just as big.

## Client Confidence

Reputation is often what brings consumers in the door. A lack of good reputation can be ruinous to a business, and there is no faster way to ruin a good reputation than to needlessly put a client's data at risk.

Many companies today hold PII that belongs to their customers. Would you expect the companies you work with to securely maintain your PII? Of course you would. The same applies in the market place. If an organization fails to properly secure data, they are leaving their customers open to many problems, and the organization is a leaving itself open to litigation and loss of reputation. Whether the data is stolen, lost, or leaked, the onus is on the custodian of the data to secure it.

The frequency and size of personal and business information leakage, whether accidental loss or deliberate theft, has seriously weakened stakeholder confidence in the information governance capabilities of both private and public sectors organizations.[2] The losses are often more than inconvenience and embarrassment, but instead carries real risks to personal welfare, organizational integrity and National security.[3]

The key attributes of a governance regime will inevitably include sensitivity, resilience, sustainability, affordability, practicality, proportionality and comprehensibility. But above all, governance must be effective and balanced, if we truly wish to preserve stakeholder confidence and trust.

## ORGANIZATIONAL TRANSPARENCY AND ACCOUNTABILITY

Being completely transparent has pros and cons. It is good for employees to understand key attributes of good governance such as responsibility, accountability, participation, and responsiveness. A company that does not consistently maintain its accountability and responsiveness leaves itself vulnerable to lawsuits, fraud charges, and loss of reputation, which can lead to a loss of business. A company that is not transparent when it should be will burn consumer (and employee) bridges, making it difficult to increase revenue and expand. Transparency in managing your data is beneficial to the extent that consumers learn to trust what you tell them. If they are concerned about data security, as most are, they know you are looking out for their best interests.

Keeping all that in mind, a balance (that word again!) must be maintained between explaining how you focus on security and not over-reporting your processes, which may have an impact on others who want to do some damage. Don't give the keys to the kingdom away in an effort to be open.

As the information governance vision takes shape for your organization, the inclusion of employees and even customers can positively affect the acceptance and successful implementation of the program. By including team members who actually use the information and do the work, you can greatly influence the outcome of the start and ongoing success of the program. Those with whom the company is engaged can evangelize the company's vision. This simple step can open doors to better employee and customer understanding of your organization. Participation allows everyone to have a voice in the process. Being transparent and open about threats and benefits will help to make the necessary changes more understandable. Also, transparency allows for enough information to be accessible to accomplish the task and to drive acceptance across the organization.[4]

Consensus orientation also recognizes the different strengths and interests of the group. Much like the concept of transparency, the intent is to keep people engaged and utilize their different skill sets and knowledge. This provides organizations the opportunity to leverage assets that they already have without having to go elsewhere to supplement their information governance needs. This also provides an opportunity for employees to take ownership of the process and the success of the team's hard work. Ownership comes in many forms. Getting people pulling in the same direction and focusing on the same goal is one form of ownership that is imperative to information governance. It is equally efficient in the use of available resources. This is where one of the favorite words of the authors comes in to play: *balance*. Balancing what needs to be done with what is reasonable is an efficient use of resources.

Accountability implements a system in which each department or person is accountable to someone. The accountability may be internal to the organization or external to stockholders or an investment group. In all cases, there needs to be accountability and systematic measurement of performance. What gets measured gets improved. If each person is willing to participate, it soon becomes standard procedure.[5]

## SIZE MATTERS

The size of the entity matters to how one enacts an information governance program. Let's look at the private, small business sector to see how technology can improve the implementation of information governance.

Small businesses or even medium-sized businesses generally have access to minimal technological assets at most. Whether these assets take the form of a friend who built the website or a contract with a graphic designer, normally the small business owner would think they were not equipped to handle any networking or information governance policies. This is simply not true and, if anything, their need is more important than that of a larger company. Target is able to recover from their breach due to their size and the resources they can apply to fixing the problem. If a small company were hit with a breach of a similar magnitude, they simply might not be able to survive the damage. Smaller companies tend to look at information governance as a lower priority than is wise. Small companies should not be afraid to be prepared.

Regardless of the size, information governance practice is important for any business. The balance for any company starts with understanding what is needed and is quickly followed by what the company can afford. There are, of course, important key attributes that can be shown to encourage businesses to embrace information governance policies. Moving toward a more comprehensive information governance strategy can help ensure the smooth flow of information through the company and even give the company a competitive edge. Besides streamlining the flow of information, proper information governance polices will also help mitigate lawsuits.

When a company has vulnerable information such as financial or competitive knowledge, it is important to keep that information safe. Failure to do so risks problems with lawsuits, regulators, or auditors. Laws and regulations dictate that certain information must be maintained under certain conditions. Proper information governance is important to stay in compliance with these laws and regulations, the failure of which can prove to be expensive through the administration of fines and penalties. When problems occur in a company and the lawyers become involved, it will be the company's policies that determine the course of action and whether or not an action was permissible. Businesses should embrace information governance policies to create an efficient flow of information and correct problems before they become lawsuits. Another one of the goals of information governance policies is to save the company money.

## MARKETING AND INFORMATION GOVERNANCE

Information governance is key in this technologically dominated business world. Companies are investing in different aspects of business practices to acquire and maintain more customers, increase revenue, and reduce costs. These practices include marketing. Frequently business entities fail to think of information governance and its impact on the marketing world. If a company can grasp the concept of what information governance is and what a positive impact it can have on sales and marketing, they can utilize the systems developed to improve their sales pitch.

Information governance should include fundamentals regarding an online presence, an online customer experience, and social media direction. Marketing in today's world has changed, and information governance is the first step in taking advantage of this burgeoning area. Most companies have a website and many have a social media focus. Ensuring the marketing is effective and serves the company goals is imperative, but a good information governance policy will also take into account security and compliance issues. You do not want to have a well-meaning yet overzealous marketer leave you susceptible to legal or access issues in the interest of expanding the business. If managing and sustaining growth are the goal, protecting that growth is just as important as implementing programs that build it.

## TECHNOLOGY ADVANCEMENTS

The use of technology has resulted in the development of new companies that are specifically geared toward implementing and teaching employers the importance of information governance. There are also organizations providing off-site physical and digital storage. Most reputable IT service providers are working with clients to find solutions to not just their technical needs but their people, compliance, and security needs. Companies are beginning to realize technology maintains information, but it is the user that manages it. People need rules to govern stipulating their responsibilities. Companies—and a large number of service providers—are recognizing that information governance adds value.

Let's take a look at the technology a company uses and how information governance can improve the effectiveness and profitability. As an example, if a brick and mortar store uses old methods such as checks, analog devices, and other dated ways of managing, the company is not profiting from more modern and efficient methods. When a company combines new and more effective means doing business—whether for making or receiving payment, ordering and controlling inventory, or managing people and payroll—the company can improve the time spent on these tasks, the preciseness of how the tasks are completed, and the security surrounding the data these tasks generate. Adding the ability to use PayPal, automating payroll, and inventory control can have an immediate positive impact on a business. The days of avoiding technology are over. The time has come to embrace technology and see it through to its fullest. Information governance helps in determining what is strategically best in the areas of technology for a business.

An additional benefit of information governance in the use of technology is the increases possible in work output. Management is, as always, a key to a smoothly running and profitable company. But management still needs guidance and vision in order to operate, elements provided by planning and communicating that vision. How are the employees going to know what to do, how to do it, and to whom to report if something goes wrong? How does an organization react to issues that can adversely impact business? How about reacting to market forces that can benefit the organization? Mismanagement can result from doing nothing and missing the road map needed to navigate through the waters of today's fast paced and ever-changing marketplace. With information governance, management is trained and given the map to work through those issues. Communication and decision-making will continue to be key to increasing the work output of the company, and a solid information governance plan helps to set the company on the right path.

By merging the key aspects of new technology with a visionary plan and straightforward policies and procedures, a company will increase its efficiency and productivity while at the same time securing its important data. This is the reality of our time. Data is in jeopardy, but there is also an opportunity to thrive with the right plan.

## INDUSTRY SPECIFICS

Let's take a look at a couple of industries to see how information governance, technology and marketing can meld and make a difference.

In the medical industry, care providers have been working toward a mandate to digitize all medical records. This allows for some excellent advantages for providers and patients. Digitized medical records—referred to as electronic medical records (EMR)—have certain positives:

- Portable medical records. Your Doctor will be able to view other caregivers' records.
- Fewer losses of records. Digital records that are backed up are safer from loss than the old system of paper records.
- Less space required, so more data can be maintained.
- Efficiency gained by quickly accessing records, history, and test results.

These are just a few of the benefits, some of which can be used to promote the business. Better efficiency and improved time management can be driven by having a system that takes advantage of improved technology. This translates into higher patient satisfaction and can be used in marketing: "a more effective way of seeing the doctor or time well spent." The improvements technology provides allows for a better-operated business, which can be further leveraged by communicating these improvements through marketing.

Are there negatives and dangers regarding the move to electronic medical records? Absolutely. The threat of data being hacked and stolen is greater, and one of the fastest growing segments of identity theft is based upon the theft of medical records. Three of the top ten places for identity theft are medically related. Health records are valuable because they contain not just the PII but the actual insurance benefits that are being stolen as well.

Information governance clearly has a place in the medical world. As we move to more and more electronic data, the threat increases—and so does complexity. With proper policy and procedures as well as employee training, the threat of loss can be mitigated but never fully removed. Additionally, as complexity increases, so does the need for rules to follow and systems to be in place to improve how effectively the data is managed, as well as how effectively patients are scheduled, treated, and processed through the medical system.

Marketing the benefits of high-performing and technically advanced facilities helps to set some organizations apart from their competitors. Medical facilities are no different. If a patient knows their appointment is going to start on time, they are much more likely to want to remain with their medical facility in the future. Electronic technology in the medical field—matched with solid information governance—is good business.

In the financial sector, the same fundamentals are true. In nearly all cases, data is kept in an electronic format. The threats are similar as well. A hack, a theft, or an error can result in devastation, and financial institutions are very high on the list of targets. Likewise, building effective solutions and utilizing modern, cutting-edge technology can reduce costs and time.

Reputation and security mean everything to banks and financial institutions. Back before technology took over the world, banks were large, imposing buildings meant to give the impression of strength and security. Why? In order to attract consumers and their money. The same applies today. Strength and security are required and need to be marketed. A hack of a financial institution could ruin a firm's reputation and result in loss of customers. Additionally, the financial industry is highly regulated. Keeping records and being able to trace and source money is a legal requirement. The data generated through clear information governance policies does just that and is the only sure way of keeping in compliance.

## ELECTRONIC DISCOVERY

Electronic discovery or e-discovery is a legal process where data is required by a judicial authority or governmental agency to be turned over to the courts, agencies, or opposition relevant to a legal or regulatory matter.

The process is not simple. Once the reporting party receives the order and the parties agree on all terms, the reporting company has to find the data, cull it to ensure only relevant data is turned over, and then deliver it in the prescribed manner. The costs of managing this process without an information governance plan can be enormous. These legal costs can be limited by having an information governance program designed to retain only the data that the business is required to maintain.

If a company's data retention plan calls for keeping everything forever, the company is putting itself at risk. Keeping unnecessary information will force the company in litigation to turn over more information than they otherwise would have been legally bound to provide. Also, legal fees are associated with document reviews, and the more information the more it will cost the company to facilitate this function.

E-discovery is a very real issue in today's world, with entire industries being built around providing only certain data—as opposed to all data—to opposing counsel. Proper governance limits the data that is maintained to strict legal standards and limits the company's legal responsibilities to only that which is required.

## COMMUNICATION

Improving communication via technology is an obvious benefit. Employees benefit by an increased understanding of internal changes and directives, which increases the productivity and overall effectiveness of the company. When communication increases, so does employee satisfaction, which in turn impacts customer satisfaction. When customer satisfaction increases, so does profitability. It is a win-win proposition that is born out of information governance through the utilization of technology to communicate most effectively.

Likewise, the ability to communication with the public can turn consumers into customers and can increase sales to people who are already buying. There is an old sales adage that says it takes six "touches" to make a sale. By automating systems and communication mechanisms, a business is able to communicate better and more frequently with its customer base and potential customers. Failing to utilize technology in the sales and marketing arena can leave a business with a sullied reputation and looking old. Consumers today have changed, and business must change with them. The newest generation with purchasing power came of age with technology involved in every facet of their lives. Business is adapting to them, and they are responding. Buying through storefronts or with old technology is disappearing quickly.

Properly leveraged information governance to implement technology into communication processes can be an extremely cost-effective means of increasing a business footprint and improving sales. In any business, there are opportunities to improve customer interaction, sometimes via people and sometimes via technology, but are often through a combination of the two. A strict, yet organized, system of interaction is driven by a solid vision, good policies, and consistent communication: in short, an information governance program.

## RISK MANAGEMENT

Improving the strength of the IT department can lead to security monitoring measures, secure connections with other institutions and customers, and secure backups of important records and data. Keeping control of business and client data is vital, and by now we all understand just how vital. In the long run, all businesses would benefit from having firm policies in place to mitigate risk and reduce cost.

Cyberliability insurance is a relatively new coverage. While it is becoming more mainstream, unfortunately many companies are ignoring the importance of having such insurance, as depicted by the chart below. However, having cyberliability coverage can prove to be well worth the expense should an organization experience a data loss.

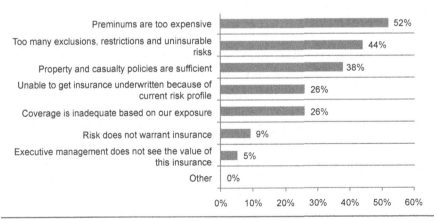

**FIGURE 9.1**    Reasons companies forego cyberliability insurance

While coverage can be designed for a particular need, as cybercoverage becomes more commonplace the policies and coverage will become more universally standard. Once more standard, it is logical to assume that such policies will require the implementation of information governance plans in order for policyholders to remain in compliance. Insurance costs will undoubtedly reflect the establishment of and adherence to these information governance plans.

There are many reasons why businesses should embrace having information governance policies. Information governance is important because the policies that a business has can determine not only how secure the business's information is but also how well the business can operate. Having solid information governance policies will help employees know how to operate in the businesses environment.

If the policy says that all data older than two years should be deleted immediately, the employees will have fewer questions about what information should be kept and what information should be destroyed or deleted. This can also help the IT department by having less data to manage, allowing them to use their time on other, more important projects. This one simple security policy can help the business through the savings of cost, time, and management of regulatory issues. A policy that states how to use a VPN or how to send information across a network can help ensure that those who want to hack or attack the network—both those outside the company as well as internal employees who should not have access to the information—cannot gain access to the information being transmitted. Information governance policies can help a business by ensuring that the information in a company is handled properly.

Information governance provides a checklist of steps that ensure security. This is also a good way to keep tabs on the business before situations get out of hand. From a purely business perspective, such diligent watchfulness on the business security and books keeps the management constantly aware of how the organization is doing. Most breaches of information are a result of the weakness or absence of basic maintenance and attention.[6]

## SEPARATION OF DATA

Security of vital and proprietary information needs to be implemented to reduce any unnecessary risks. Different levels of data importance will drive different levels of security. While there should always be a baseline of security, more sensitive data requires a higher threshold. Though some companies may decide that the cost for such security is not worth the insurance it would provide them in the long term, the question needs to be evaluated closely.

An excellent example is the 2013 Target store breach. Target customers suffered from the breach and Target suffered losses in client loyalty, penalties, and multiple class-action lawsuits. The actual cost to Target has not yet been fully determined, but it is safe to say that in the final analysis the cost will be in the billions of dollars.

It is not difficult to imagine that Target might have taken some different steps to have been better prepared for cyberattacks. Can a company stop every attack, every time? No, but companies can ensure that they are doing everything possible to be a good custodian of their clients' data.

In today's technologically advanced society, more and more threats are being developed for organizations that rely on networks with access to the Internet. In actuality, many businesses utilize technology and the Internet without understanding the risks involved. Spending the time and money to develop the necessary information governance systems to prepare and protect your data is worth every cent. Conversely, it can be time and money the company will wish it had spent after they are attacked. As the old saying goes, "If you fail to prepare you are preparing to fail."

Major corporations are being held accountable for any private information that is leaked or stolen by hackers or other means. In 2011, Sony's PlayStation Network was hacked and the personal information of about seventy-seven million customers was stolen. This caused major problems for the company and resulted in market-share loss, reputational loss and revenue loss. Amazingly enough, all of this damage was caused not by some sophisticated criminal syndicate, but rather by a lone college student.

Other companies have almost been put out of business, if not completely ruined, by disgruntled employees who were angry or disenchanted. The managers and human resources failed to revoke the employee's ability to access the company's computer system when he or she was discharged, and the employee deleted and/or stole important information that belonged to the company. In what is referred to as ransomware, there have been instances where an individual, often overseas, holds a computer hostage with the use of a virus. They lock users out of the system or take the data and demand to be paid a ransom to unlock the computer or return the data. Instances like these are why all companies should have an information governance plan in place to help prevent information from being leaked or stolen, and to provide a plan of what actions to take should the worst occur.

## LEGAL

Electronic Discovery is not the only legal issue businesses face when not prepared. Companies have legal obligations dictated by federal and state law to protect employee and consumer PII.

Negligence can mean people are personally and perhaps even criminally liable. Do not take data management for granted. Ask the tough questions. Ask those who are the keepers of the data. Find ways to protect yourself and your business. People are attempting to do harm to your business on a daily basis, and issues arise for which the company must be prepared. From a legal perspective, information governance encourages the consistent handling of sensitive information.

A system to grade preparedness—like a Good Housekeeping seal of approval—would be highly beneficial in mitigating legal liability. Companies could earn a rating based on how they employ and enforce their policies, and how well their employees are educated. Having this in place would also benefit the customers of these companies, who would know their information is being protected and held to an industry standard.

Additionally, having such a rating could possibly deter hackers and others from attempting to exploit systems. In security, it is called target hardening. Companies want their systems to be more secure than someone else's so that the hacker will move on to the weaker system. Think of it like taking a hike in the woods with someone else. If you get attacked by a bear on the hike, you don't need to out run the bear; you only need to out run the other person.

## SELLING YOUR COMPANY ON THE IDEA OF INFORMATION GOVERNANCE

The business world of today relies heavily on technology. Information governance is an organization's effort to manage information by implementing controls, records, processes, and guidelines that help a business run securely and efficiently. The strategies employed can help a company battle the forces trying to take advantage of the data, and assist in making the business a more effective, efficient, and profitable entity.

In this chapter, a few simple strategies have been identified, but the bottom line involves thinking through the issues for your particular company and determining what is a good and reasonable means to protect it and improve your organization. This is not rocket science. Most of information governance is common sense and awareness. The trick is in the implementation. Plan. Do. Review. Redo. Repeat.

## References

1. SAP Group, "Making Information Governance a Reality for Your Organization," December 2011, p. 9, accessed January 2014. http://www.sapexecutivenetwork.com/files/Making_Information_Governance_a_Reality_for_Your_Organization_(en).pdf.
2. Colin Beveridge, "The Better Practice Forum, Information Governance: Measures for Preserving Stakeholder Confidence," October 2008, p. 4, accessed January 2014. http://www.eurim.org.uk/activities/ig/Measures_for_preserving_stakeholder_confidence.pdf.
3. Ibid.
4. Hari Srinivas, United Nations Development Program, Urban Governance; governance for sustainable human development, January 4, 2014.
5. Robert D. Behn, "Why Measure Performance? Different Purposes Require Different Measures," *Public Administration Review* 63, no. 5 (2003): http://dx.doi.org/10.1111/1540-6210.00322.
6. Barclay T. Blair, "8 Reasons Why Information Governance (IG) Makes Sense," *Association for Information and Image Management Blog*, June 29, 2009, accessed January 2014. http://aiim.typepad.com/aiim_blog/2009/06/8-reasons-why-information-governance-ig-makes-sense.html.

# Chapter 10

# What to do First

Technology plays a major role in today's businesses, which means more than ever a solid information governance plan is a necessity. However, in the business world, while technology has been advancing for decades, the concept of information governance has gotten off to a slow start. Most companies have done very little—if anything at all—to set policies to protect their business.

## The Basics

In a survey conducted by the Economist Intelligence Unit, "77% of respondents expect information governance to be important or very important to their company's success."[1] Yet, only 51 percent of respondents indicated that the companies for whom they worked had a formal information governance strategy.[2] This survey indicates that although most understand the importance of information governance, few have taken the necessary steps to ensure implementation.

**137**

## First Things First

If your organization is going to have comprehensive and successful information governance plan, the first step will be to establish a committee to oversee the development and implementation of these policies. The persons who are on this committee, along with the person appointed to be in charge will be critical in the eventual outcome of the polices that are developed.

The goal of the information governance committee would be to research the issues that need to be addressed, as well as brainstorm other potential issues that can pose threats to information governance.

The leader of the information governance committee should not necessarily be someone affiliated with the company's IT functions. It is important to remember that information governance is much more than just protecting data from loss; it is also about being able to access information as needed and facilitating a business to its most productive and profitable levels. Accordingly, whoever is chosen to the lead the committee should have a solid understand of the organization's place in the business world and what is needed for the company to operate successfully. Armed with this information, the leader can guide the committee toward finding solutions that will protect the company's interests without inhibiting operations.

Whoever is chosen as the leader will also need to have a proverbial seat at the table. The leader of the information governance committee needs to be able to report to the top, providing insight as to the threats and the changes that need to be implemented. Too often, those in charge of information governance are too far down the chain, often reporting to others whose job it is to then report to the higher executives. With such a hierarchy, the necessity or urgency of policy change and implementation is frequently watered down. If companies are serious about embracing the incorporation of information governance, they need to demonstrate this by ensuring the committee leader has direct access to the top of the decision chain and that those at the top of this chain welcome these briefings.

After identifying who should be the leader, this individual should have free rein to recruit persons from various areas of the company who can bring different perspectives of what is needed and what can be accomplished. This team can come from any facet of the organization, but consideration should be given to persons form both human resources and legal in order to take advantage of their competence in addressing any potential impact on employee rights or the law.

It should go without saying that a representative of the IT department should be part of this committee. Too often, IT is either relegated to being solely responsible for implementing information governance or not included at all in the thought process during development. IT can address many of the major issues, but others will be needed for those issues that are not directly impacted or controlled by technology. Social engineering is not the sole domain of the Internet, so those in sales or a call center may have valuable input as well.

## DETERMINE YOUR COMPANY'S NEEDS

In establishing an information governance program for your company, you will need to take the time to properly determine exactly what your company's needs are. No one size fits all when it comes to protecting valuable data, so it will be incumbent upon the information governance committee to determine how much security will be needed and exactly what steps should be taken to protect the information in question.

First and foremost, it is important to understand what type of information the company deals with and the amount of risk associated with the information. As was stated in Chapter 9, the size of the company and the scale of the possible threat should determine the financial commitment that will be necessary. On the other hand, a small company could be working on particular sensitive information, such as a defense contractor working on projects for the United States government. Even though they are a small company, their mission may demand the very best of what a solid information governance program may have to offer.

The information governance committee would to have properly defined the company's business objectives. There needs to be a baseline of what the company is hoping to achieve by setting up and defining an information governance program, including why the company believes such a program is needed and what level of resources—both in people and in monetary assets—the company is willing to invest to meet the objective. Likewise, in establishing this baseline, the information governance committee will also need to determine what is already being done by the organization, as well as what level of information security knowledge is possessed by the existing employees. Of course the best way to determine the answer to this last question is simply to ask those within the company what they are already doing.

If the company is small enough, it may be possible to question each individual on their security habits and their level of knowledge when it comes to information security. For larger corporations, this would not necessarily be practical, but the information governance committee can still take steps to interview department managers and perhaps have employees complete a corporate survey of their information governance practices. Having a baseline of how much you need to educate will provide the committee a good basis as to where to begin.

One of the things the information governance committee will need to do is make a determination of the organization's assets. Different businesses will have different assets. An electronics producer's assets could include its product blueprints, customers, and its computer systems, whereas a major clothing retailer's assets could include its product, financial data, and social media. In determining the company's assets, it is important to include an examination of the organization's physical equipment, software, the company's work activities, the employees, partners, and its customers, all in the interest of establishing where breaches of good information governance practices might occur.

The software programs the organization may be using to accomplish their mission can be of particular importance. How are these programs being utilized to store information safely? As programs are updated with new versions, will these newer versions enable the organization to retriever older files and open them, or do stored files need to be re-saved under the new format so that they may be reviewed later. Think of all the files that just years ago were saved under programs like WordPerfect, while today the standard off-the-shelf word processing program is Microsoft Word. These two programs are generally not compatible, making it difficult for a document prepared in one program to be read properly by another.

In addition to corporate documents, the information governance committee should look at related areas of interest such as e-mails, Internet usage, the use of both personal and business phones and computers, the ability of employees to work from home, and their potential for taking proprietary work outside of the company to an off-site location.

## METHODS OF SECURITY

Once the level of information governance policies an organization requires has been established, consideration should be given to the various methods of security that are available to achieve the objective.

Rather than reinventing the wheel, it might be wise to look at similar businesses that are successful and examine what steps they have taken to incorporate information governance into their business practices. This is not to say that other businesses should be copied exactly, because the needs of each business will vary based upon mission objectives, resources, and people. However, much can be learned by studying what has worked for others, taking advantages of the policies that might benefit your organization, and customizing those policies to have them fit your organization's needs.

The information governance committee will need to develop a list of priorities covering the various areas of the company where information governance should be implemented. As discussed in Chapter 8, it is probably best to implement changes a little at a time in order not to create too much distraction from the main focus of the company's business objective. Therefore, when introducing information governance policies piecemeal, the information governance committee should ascertain what methods of security are the priorities and what should therefore be implemented first to afford the organization the maximum beneficial impact.

For example, if the company is not backing up their documents to an off-site storage facility, this might be of greater importance than implementing procedures that control physical access. While keeping persons out who do not belong is an excellent objective, problems can take a variety of forms other than physical access (e.g. computer intrusion, equipment failure, etc. Better to ensure the information has been safely secured to protect against all of these threats before opting to make changes that protect against just one possible compromise.

Once the information governance committee is confident that they have identified the significant risks, the committee must then consider measures of implementation that eradicate the risk or substantially mitigates the threat. Different risks will require different techniques to mitigate them. Accordingly, companies will find that these techniques vary from physical to digital. A physical example of eliminating or mitigating risks would be the use of security guards, alarms, and cameras to monitor the organization's facilities. On the other hand, a digital example of would be the utilization of firewalls, antivirus software, intrusion detection systems, and so on.

Finally, although it may not at first appear to be obvious, another issue regarding methods of security is to make sure that the organization's upper management has accountability in the implementation process. By having the policy implementations openly discussed, disseminated, and supported by those in charge, the chance that the new information governance policies will be pushed off to the side is reduced. The importance of these policies needs to be emphasized along with a sense of urgency. Open recognition by persons in authority of the importance of the policies can diminish breaches in the efficiency and security of the policy implementation.

## PLAN SECURITY METHODS AND SYSTEMS

When developing information governance security plans, it is a good idea not only to take a look at what needs to be made secure but also to take into consideration what does not. Does all of the information in your organization need to be retained forever, or is their information that can be discarded after a period of time? If retained, can the storage of this information be done less expensively than more sensitive data because its loss would not be problematic for the company?

Personal information pertaining to prior employees may not need to be readily available and might be removed from the main computer systems. However, the personal information of even former employees should be considered sensitive, and steps must be taken to safeguard this data. In cases of where physical records exist, consideration should be given to condensing information by scanning documents or eliminating physical records when electronic records already exist. The elimination of unnecessary physical records not only decreases the chance of unintended exposure but can also reduce costs in the saving of space and storage. When disposing physical copies of such information, it highly recommended that everything be shredded rather than just tossed in the trash. Good information governance practices should always be applied to all types of sensitive information, even that which you no longer need.

In some instances, blocking access to electronic files can be accomplished by limiting which computers within the company are exposed to the Internet. Some systems may be able to be designated as solely internal and be accessed on stand-alone computers (i.e., computers that have no connectivity to anything other than the internal network). By the creation of a system of stand-alone computers for internal records, the possibility of information loss due to a computer intrusion has effectively been eliminated. To achieve this properly, the organization would most likely have to facilitate hosting a private network within the company by having their own server. Granted, additional costs are associated with doing this—both in finances and IT personnel resources to maintain the system—but the potential benefits to be gained by the company may well be worth it in the long run.

Likewise, in some instances organizations may wish to take this policy even one step further by prohibiting the use of flash drives on the stand-alone units. By doing so, the ability to have malware inadvertently loaded onto the system has also been eliminated, thereby protecting your internal system data from possible corruption or destruction.

Another method of security is to institute a need-to-know policy. Not all employees need or should have access to all systems. Employees in human resources should have access to personnel data, the company's health office will have access to employee medical records, and corporate engineers will have access to proprietary design information. However, unless a logical argument can be made otherwise, there should be no reason for the crossover of information from one of these departments to another. By maintaining the need to know rule, important information will not be shared with those who should not have access, and the potential for unnecessary spillage will be greatly reduced. Employees should have access to only the information they need to perform their jobs. Anything beyond this is unnecessary and creates potential information security problems.

## CREATION OF THE INFORMATION GOVERNANCE POLICIES

Having assessed the organization and determined its information governance needs, it is time to create the policies that put the necessary guidance into place. The information governance committee will take the lead, but to develop effective policies you are going to need to retain the assistance of those in charge of the various departments within your organization. This is one of the reasons it is a good idea to have the information governance committee comprise representatives from several different departments, so that these individuals can liaison with their respective groups and report back with suggestions of what is needed and how it can be achieved. Another benefit of working with the other departments is that when it comes time to implement the new information governance policies, the committee will already have buy-in from those who will be affected.

When developing policies that involve electronic data, such as the case of the stand-alone computer server, it is important to make sure IT is brought into the discussion early on. The lion's share of the electronic efforts will fall upon IT, so efforts need to be made to ensure that the desired policies are possible. Likewise, for these policies to be put into practice, IT will need to have the dedicated resources to do so, both in finances and manpower. If more money or employees are required, it should be the job of the information governance committee to make the case for such, rather than have the IT personnel enter these battles on their own.

The development of information governance policies will be tailored to the individual needs of each company or organization. Information is not a one-size-fits-all process, which is why input from all departments is so important. However, in the world of information governance, a few things are standard with most company policies. Here are just a few examples.

To protect proprietary information, it is generally a good idea for companies to incorporate non-compete and "do not disclose" clauses into their employee contracts. This way, when an employee leaves the company—voluntarily or through termination—the restrictions placed upon the employee to protect the company will remain.

Information governance polices should always address password changes, generally requiring they be changed every three months to ensure a proper level of security. Additionally, the policy will should also incorporate language that calls for the immediate rescinding of the password the moment the employee departs from the company, if not sooner (such as when they provide their notice).

Software updates should be part of the information governance strategy. By outlining the requirement that the most up-to-date software be utilized on the organization's computer system that connects to the Internet, the company will ensure they have the latest versions that account for all known viruses and threats.

While it would be nice for information governance policies to mitigate every single risk using every measure possible, in reality this cannot always be done. The reality of today's business world is that all organizations will have a certain amount of limitations, including cost, time, personnel resources, and more. If a business has to purchase new and expensive equipment, but cannot afford to do so, they have no choice but to look elsewhere for possible solutions. Likewise, some companies may have difficulties with the implementation of new technologies simply because it is not economically feasible for the computers to go offline for the amount of time it would take to install updated systems.

Where the preferred fixes are not available, the potential problems should still not be ignored. Rather, organizations should take into account their limitations and look at other avenues they can take. For example, if it is not possible to update to a new version of software, employees should be made aware of the threat issues that are found within the version they are using so that they can be on the lookout for any anomalies.

Additionally, some companies might never before have considered having a full time chief information security officer as part of the corporate structure. In Appendix A, the authors have included and outline of what qualifications a potential candidate might have for such a position. Likewise, to get those on the information governance committee thinking more specifically about the issues that need to be addressed in their policies, the authors have also included templates for information governance threat assessment (Appendix B) and information governance threat response planning (Appendix C).

## IMPLEMENTATION

In a setting where an organization had not previously had any established information governance policies, once the need for such is discovered, the inclination would be to thrust upon the employees all protective provisions as soon as feasible. As well intentioned as this might seem, it is human nature to reject change, at least initially. The newly established information governance policies will likely at first appear to be cumbersome. As stated earlier, a more gradual rollout of new policies might prove to be most effective. The gradual introduction of information governance policies will permit employees the opportunity to learn and understand what they need to do in order to be in compliance, and to have a better understanding of why these policies are import to their company's success.

In advance of implementing information governance policies, it is important to have a plan to educate everyone within the organization of what is to be expected. Doing so will not only reduce the confusion that generally accompanies the introduction of new procedures but also provide the opportunity to encourage employees to embrace the coming changes. Whether via e-mail, team meetings, or even one-on-one sessions, communicating the importance and benefits of the information governance policies allows the implementation process to occur with the least amount of difficulties.

Make sure that all of the employees whom the new information governance policies will directly affect are made aware of these changes in advance and given at least a general idea of why the changes are being instituted. People especially dislike change when they do not understand the reasons behind it. If possible, announce the coming changes to everyone in a physical environment so that employees have a chance to ask questions and listen to other questions they had not thought of themselves.

When educating those who will be affected by the changes, the more details the better. In addition to meeting in person, also develop an office memo detailing the what, when, and why. This memo should not just detail the security strengths of the company but also address the existing weaknesses and explain how information governance will strengthen the organization against the variety of potential threats.

Likewise, both the meeting and the memo should challenge employees to become an active part of the equation by encouraging and rewarding them for identifying other potential threats and viable solutions.

The final step of implementing information governance policies is to establish a working system that utilizes the policies. At this stage, all the steps that were identified and adopted will now be put into practice, rolled out progressively based on their importance and substantive impact. Having employees sign non-disclosure agreements might allow management to feel that something had been accomplished, but perhaps the more immediate threat would be to address holes in the computer network that need to be patched. Additionally, some elements of information governance lend themselves to implementation during specific periods of the company's fiscal year. For example, the time of the annual employee reviews would provide an ideal occasion to discuss non-disclosure and non-compete provisions of the organization's information governance policies. Employees could be provided copies of these policies, given an opportunity to review, and then asked to sign them, whereupon the signed copies would be collected and made part of the employee's human resources file. Eventually, an overview of the entire information governance policy should be incorporated into the employee's annual review in the form of a written acknowledgement of the policies that the employee will sign and date. Doing so not only reiterates for the employee the importance of information governance but also provides the organization with legal recourse should an employee's intentional breach of a policy prove detrimental to the organization.

As part of the implementation of these policies, specific individuals at various levels of authority within the organization would be assigned to track the use of the policies and to ensure that they are being utilized properly and effectively. For example, security personnel can send out reminders of online threats, such as malware. Comprehension of the policies can be established through the administration of occasional short tests that measure the employees' understanding and practice of the policies. Eventually, security may even wish to send fake e-mails to random groups of employees to test their ability to recognize threats.

Individual departments or sections of the company should be briefed on any specific changes that will affect their work. This will provide employees a further opportunity to digest what is expected and how they may meet these expectations. By definition, those in the IT department who manage the various organizational electronic systems may be called upon more than others to implement changes. IT employees are the ultimate keepers of the stored information, but their already demanding jobs can be made easier by the overall education of employees, ensuring they understand basic practices such as password security and social engineering avoidance.

Much of the education of employees can be achieved through mandatory classes on information governance, which can be held on specific training days. Employees need to know more than just the fact that new policies are being put into place. They need to understand how to recognize suspicious activities and to whom they should report their observations.

How much training should be offered depends on the type and volume of policies that are being put into effect. Training should be developed for all of the intended policies, and a training schedule should be developed to coincide with the implementation of these policies. Additionally, it would be beneficial to have these training programs led—or at least introduced—by a high-ranking official within the organization in order to convey the importance of learning these policies and procedures.

Likewise, employees can be reassured that although information governance policies may appear to be intimidating at the outset, after time they will seem second nature. If the information governance policies are implemented in an organized step-by-step manner, the perception of value within the organization will become apparent, thereby further encouraging persons to engage in their own efforts to ensure security. With each additional employee willingly participating in their specific function of information governance a step is taken toward the policies becoming standard procedures throughout the company. And, as we have learned early on, consistent standard procedure adds to consumer and employee confidence.

## EVALUATE EFFECTIVENESS AND REVISE POLICIES

Once all the information governance measures have been implemented, it is useful to monitor the performance and effectiveness of the new policies. By doing so, the organization can ensure that the desired result of managing and protecting the company's important information has been achieved. If one or more information governance policies is determined to be ineffective, such policies can be amended or removed, depending upon the expected results.

Additionally, information governance is a continually evolving program, changing as technology and business needs change. Information governance policies should be a flexible system that can adapt to future changes in the company's industry. Making sure the policies are working and offering solutions to possible issues is the continuing job of the information governance committee.[3]

Any newly developed policies will undoubtedly become stale and outdated over time. After implementation, employees should be encouraged to provide input regarding their perceptions of how the policies are working and their thoughts on how policies might be changed. Doing so will significantly enhance the organization's ability to identify information governance security issues and stay ahead of developing problems.

For example, during the period of employee feedback, a determination may be made that one policy contradicts another. During this evaluation period, changes can be made to ensure the more necessary policy remains in place while determining the necessity of the other policy. Adjustments can be made to avoid the overlap, or the other policy can be eliminated completely.

Companies should also assess how employees are adapting to the new policies. Are employees able to conform easily to the policies? Are there any notable changes in productivity or efficiency? The company should make sure its employees are following the information governance policies and establish remediation processes to help employees who are having difficulties. Understanding how the work force is reacting to the newly established information governance policies makes it easy to pinpoint what works and what does not, and thereby make adjustments to keep the company safe and secure.

## SOME ADDITIONAL THOUGHTS

One often-overlooked aspect of a good information governance plan is the establishment of outside relationships and contacts with those who could help during an event. Part of the organization's plan should be to know whom to contact within law enforcement and to establish a liaison to this contact within your organization. The first time you speak with the police or the FBI should not be when you need their assistance. Getting to know these individuals in advance and discussing information governance can be extremely beneficial in determining the outcome of your event.

Implementing information governance is a critical aspect of any business, but it can also be a tedious and sometimes daunting task. It can prove useful, therefore, to create an outline of how a company should establish information governance for the first time. For convenience, what follows is a list of a few of the things that should be considered:

## How to Determine Information Governance Needs for Your Company

- Determine the risk verses the reward.
- Decide how much you can spend for what you can obtain.
- Weigh the need for client confidence verses unintended disclosure.
- Examine what threats are realistic.
- Determine how you should manage your electronic and physical information.
- Determine who can have access to information and at what level.
- Decide how you will inventory the company's assets and how often.
- Determine what needs you have for physical security.
- Decide who will have authority over enforcement of information governance policies.
- Assess your need for retrieving information if you are involved in litigation.
- Have buy-in by important personnel at the start (e.g., CEO, financial, legal, HR, CIO, IT, etc.)

# How to Create Information Governance Policies

- Talk to all employees about information governance, explaining its importance.
- Develop clearly defined rules about consequences for violating information governance policies.
- Put firewalls in place.
- Implement password protection (i.e., require changes at set intervals).
- Determine who can handle what information (need-to-know).
- Establish rules for taking work home.
- Decide how you will store electronic and physical information safely and securely.
- Establish a baseline of information governance practices.
- Develop industry- and department-specific policies depending on threat level.
- Have the information governance committee—in conjunction with legal, IT, HR, and employee groups—determine what the best practices, policies, and procedures should be

# Methods of Security to Support Information Governance

**Hardware:**

- USB authentication
- Backup servers
- Approved devices
- Fingerprint scanners
- Offsite backup
- Multiple internet access points
- Multiple power sources
- Backup generators
- "Bring your own device" (BYOD) policy
- Standardized user security suites
- Firewalls
- Server log activity tracking
- Wi-Fi encryption
- non-technical solution where appropriate

**Software:**

- Forced password reset
- Security questions
- Caption picture
- Firewalls

- antispyware and antivirus
- Device blocker
- Idle logout
- Ping database
- Website blocking
- Keystroke tracker

**Automated:**

- Auto update
- Auto scan
- Auto authentication check
- Auto quarantine threat
- Auto log IP address

# How to Implement Information Governance Policies

**Small Business:**

- Memo to all employees
- All-employee meeting
- Employee questions and answers
- Follow-up reminder e-mails
- IT involvement
- Up-to-date knowledge of current laws and regulations
- Clearly defined rules about consequences for breaking information governance policies
- Firewalls
- Password protection
- Rules about what information can be handled by which employees
- Training, both initial and annual
- Awareness programs
- Different levels of focus for different risk levels

**Medium-Size Business:**

- Memo to all employees
- All-employee meeting
- Employee questions and answers
- Follow-up reminder e-mails
- IT involvement
- Up-to-date knowledge of current laws and regulations

- Clearly defined rules about consequences for breaking information governance policies
- Firewalls
- Password protection
- Rules about what information can be handled by which employees
- Guidelines established for employees
- Training exercises
- IT involvement
- Clearly defined information governance leaders
- Cheerleaders

**Large Business:**

- Memo to all employees
- All-employee meeting
- Employee questions and Answers
- Follow-up reminder e-mails
- IT involvement
- Up-to-date knowledge of current laws and regulations
- Clearly defined rules about consequences for breaking information governance policies
- Firewalls
- Password protection
- Rules about what information can be handled by which employees
- Guidelines established for employees
- Training exercises
- IT involvement
- Non-disclosure agreements
- Recurrent, annual review
- "Bring your own device" (BYOD) policy
- Standardized security suites
- Establishment of a high level information governance committee
- Integrity testing
- Employee quizzes
- Follow-up employee meetings
- Tighter security protocols depending on level of employee involvement
- Communication

Where sensitive data exists, there will be a need to ensure the data is protected. IT alone can only do so much, hence the need for participation by everyone in the company. Policies can be developed that limit access, and policies can be developed to offer protections to information being accessed. The implementation of a solid information governance plan is a way to ensure that everyone understand his or her responsibility in protecting the organization's most important asset.

## References

1. Economist Intelligence Unit, "The Future of Enterprise Information Governance," October 2008, p. 2, accessed January 2014. http://www.emc.com/collateral/analyst-reports/economist-intell-unit-info-governence.pdf.
2. Ibid, p. 3.
3. SAP Group, "Making Information Governance a Reality for Your Organization," December 2011, p. 5, accessed January 2014. http://www.sapexecutivenetwork.com/files/Making_Information_Governance_a_Reality_for_Your_Organization_(en).pdf.

# Chapter 11

# What to do Forever

By this point, we have identified what information governance is, what it means to your company, what your company does not have in place, and what your company needs. Committees have been developed, personnel assigned tasks, and queries made to determine security gaps. Policies have been created and implemented. Technology in the form of both hardware and software has been purchased and put into action to assist with protecting your organization's important information. Employees have been explained the importance of information governance, and training has been conducted to ensure the proper education of all personnel. So what is left to do? Plenty.

## Continuing Efforts

Information governance is now—and forever will remain—an evolving process. As technology changes, so will the potential threats, which means that it is incumbent upon organizations to stay abreast of these changes in order to protect their valuable data. After the policies are outlined, a system should be put in place to evaluate, to receive feedback, and then to act on the feedback to have the best results with information governance.

Technology is now changing exponentially. Developments in technology are coming into existence faster than ever before, and what we view today as being fast will be considered slow in just a year or two. In the course of normal job responsibilities, your IT personnel will become aware of many of these developments, which is why these employees play such a critical role in your information governance program. Likewise, those assigned to the information governance committee, in particular your company's chief information officer, should make it part of their mission to continually educate themselves on developments in the field of information governance protections and threats.

Even companies that are in the specific business of protecting sensitive information might not be doing all they can. In Peters v. LifeLock, Michael Peters, Life-Lock's former chief information security officer, alleged that his risk assessment revealed that the company was performing only 27 percent of the minimum intrusion prevention, data leakage and encryption, and other technological security readiness measures needed to protect its customers' sensitive information.[1] Mr. Peters claims he also discovered that LifeLock had not dedicated any internal resources to security vigilance measures, including vulnerability testing, auditing or monitoring, incident management, and event logging.[2]

Beyond awareness of the changes, threats, and solutions, there are actions that companies should employ as part of their information governance program to ensure continued advancement of their organization's policies so that they remain current as the world continues to evolve.

## CONTINUING EFFORTS OF THE INFORMATION GOVERNANCE COMMITTEE

Once the policies have been developed and implemented, there is still plenty for the information governance committee to continue to do. This committee should remain a permanent fixture of the organizational structure and continue to have the ability to report to the highest levels of the company in order for information governance to play a defensive role in all aspects of the company's affairs.

The committee members are the members of the organization that should evaluate whether the information governance policies are being implemented correctly and followed properly. It is equally important that employees feel empowered to provide feedback on the effectiveness of the policies. Each department of an organization should have a representative available to meet with the committee to present problems or solutions that were developed during the course of their work. And all persons should continue to have unfettered access to share their information governance observations.

As technology changes, so should the makeup of the membership of the committee. By members occasionally rotating on and off the committee, new members will be afforded direct exposure to the importance of this program and will bring fresh perspectives and different points of view. This may enhance existing policies, but may also more easily facilitate the development of new protocols that are needed. Logically, while the committee should have regularly scheduled meetings, with subsequent reporting to the company executives, should a significant risk be discovered, an emergency meeting should be convened in order for the necessary protective actions to be put into place as soon as possible. Additionally, should an operational need or process improvement be identified, it would be important for the committee to meet. The committee must be driven to keep abreast of changes and to look not only for security issues but also areas that can be improved.

## ACCOUNTABILITY

If policies have been properly disseminated and employees have been properly trained, the organization's personnel need to be accountable for abiding by information governance protocols.

This is not to suggest that employees should necessarily be punished for failures in following information governance protocols, although in certain instances some sort of formal discipline may be appropriate, such as in the case of repeated breaches due to inattentiveness. Obviously any willful act is grounds for serious discipline. Otherwise, the overseers should monitor accountability by employees, and employers should view lapses as opportunities for improvement.

In cases involving minor offenses resulting in little or no damage to data, offenders can be afforded additional training and counseling by their superiors to explain the needs of the corporate information governance policies further. In many cases, the employees may be aware of the policies, but may not have an actual understanding of how adherence protects the organization. An employee who does not understand malware is not going to understand the dangers associated with using an unapproved flash drive. In this instance, education can be the cure. An educated employee is far more apt to be a cautious employee, and an accountable employee is far more likely to keep focus on the policies.

On occasion, employees will knowingly violate policies even though they possess an understanding of the reasons for the information governance protocols. Whether due to laziness or something far more nefarious, employees who willingly put the corporate data at risk must be addressed. The manner by which to address these instances may be tiered, from education to admonishment to discipline and finally to dismissal. The punishment level would vary depending upon the severity of the breach and the rationale of the employee responsible.

Accountability affords an organization the opportunity to maintain awareness of how effective the information governance security policies are. Employees who are identified as being intentional or unintentional weak links in corporate security can be reassigned if necessary in an effort to minimize potential damage. The company will also know of additional steps to take, such as retraining. Likewise, having accountability affords the opportunity to further identify offenders on the outside who seek to exploit these weaknesses, allowing an organization not only the opportunity to stop the attackers but also to report them as necessary to the authorities.

In the business world, new risks, threats, and exploits happen every day. The policies that employees were trained on yesterday may no longer work today or tomorrow. Therefore, organizations must understand that although employees should be accountable, successful attacks against potential weaknesses might not necessarily be the employees' fault.

## CONTINUED TRAINING

As previously mentioned above, there are occasions when a select number of personnel may require remedial training to become as proficient as others within the organization. Nevertheless, all employees—no matter how proficient they may be—are going to need periodical refresher training. The longer people work in an environment, the more they get comfortable and become complacent. The more complacent the employee, the easier they are to exploit. Give employees reminders of the policies through e-mails, posters on the company walls, and any other means available.

Continued training provided by the employer is the best way to ensure the company's information governance policies are continued and enhanced. Training days should be established periodically throughout the year—or at the very minimum at least once a year. Dedicating an entire day to various concerns in not necessary, but investing as little as an hour on thoughtful education of information governance policies can prove to be time well spent in the protection of sensitive data. Likewise, these training opportunities can be in many forms, from an all-employee meeting for the sole purpose of discussing information governance to more informal settings of department managers meeting with the personnel in their charge.

Continued training serves several purposes. Employees can be reminded about what they have been previously taught, allowing the organization to ensure that the information remains current in the employee's mind. Likewise, it reminds the employee of the importance of the topic, helping to prevent the employee from becoming careless in the handling of sensitive information.

Additionally, the continued education provides an opportunity to share with employees the latest developments—including both new threats and new solutions that have been developed to combat those threats. As new risks arise, these issues can be incorporated into the company's information governance policies, and employee will have the necessary confidence to be prepared for the risks that potentially threaten their information.

## PERIODIC TESTING

There is an old Russian proverb famously used by Ronald Reagan during his presidency: "Trust yet verify." An organization can offer all of the training in the world, but at some point they will want to make sure that it is actually working. There are many ways to put a company's information governance policies to the test.

In the corporate world, computer penetration testing—often known as pen testing—is a common practice. After firewalls and other software fixes are put into place to keep out the criminals, organizations can hire companies that will act as the bad guys and attempt to hack into the computer system. If they are able to conduct a successful computer intrusion, the organization will have the information they need to put patches into place. Conversely, if the pen testers are unsuccessful, the organization will have confidence in their established protections, at least until smarter criminals come along who possess a higher level of skill. Pen testing should be conducted periodically to ensure the best possible protections are put into place.

Pen testing is a means to test the physical equipment, but as discussed throughout this book, employees also pose various levels of threats to their employer's sensitive information. Some of the ways to test an employee's knowledge and training include sending them an e-mail that might be considered a use of social engineering. Whether phishing for information directly or seeking access to the computer system by obtaining passwords, social engineering tests can identify gaps in training and places where resources need to be directed to fill these gaps.

Beyond computers, employee testing can also be conducted in the form of ruse telephone calls seeking inside information from an employee by pretending to be a higher up in the corporation. If the employee follows the appropriate verification protocols, perhaps they can be rewarded, providing an incentive for all employees to be just as cautious. If the employee fails the test, education and retraining can be offered to correct problems.

## TECHNOLOGICAL UPGRADES

According to the Lillian Ablon, et al., sophisticated and specialized markets that freely deal in the tools and the spoils of cybercrime have assisted the growth in cybercrime. These include items such as exploit kits (software tools that can help create, distribute, and manage attacks on systems), botnets (a group of compromised computers remotely controlled by a central authority that can be used to send spam or flood websites), as-a-service models (hacking for hire), and the fruits of cybercrime, including stolen credit card numbers and compromised hosts.[3]

New technology can facilitate new business opportunities and possibly less expensive operational expenses. But new technology can also bring an increased exposure to potential risks by criminals taking advantage of these new technologies.

To protect against these new threats, companies must stay up-to-date with their information governance policy as it pertains to the incorporation of new technologies. The policies must address the new technologies that pose the threats.

The business world relies heavily on technology. Today, most companies use some form of digital information management system involving both hardware and software. These systems need to be maintained and updated on a regular basis. In addition to addressing how new technologies are used within the organization, information governance policies must also cover the maintenance and upgrading of these systems throughout the organization.

Updating hardware can be expensive. Replacing all of the computer systems that sits on of each employee's desk is no small task. However, at a certain point in the life of hardware, technology equipment becomes so out-of-date that security precautions are more difficult to implement. Hardware can also reach a point where it is unable to address today's threats. The financial investment made to upgrade hardware when necessary may prove to be a significant cost savings in the long run by preventing the potential disaster of sensitive information being lost, stolen, or altered.

Software also needs to be regularly updated to address the latest threats as they arise. Good information governance protocols will require the immediately download of updates provided by the vendor, as these updates usually fix vulnerabilities to their systems.

Likewise, other software programs such as antispyware and virus protection should be updated whenever new versions are available in order to fend off the latest malware that has been released on the Internet. This can also be done at little cost to the company by conducting an automatic daily update of virus protection software. This automatic update can be conducted during nonbusiness hours to avoid disrupting business operations. This simple step will greatly ensure the organization's overall computer security is current and up-to-date.

Finally, the technological aspects of the information governance policy should also address what must occur should malware or another threat successfully penetrate the company's computer network. The policies would outline who should receive notification, what steps will be taken to contain the threat from spreading and removing it from the system, and how the threat may be blocked from further action in the future. Planning for prevention and addressing threats as they occur are important, as is ensuring this same threat is not unwittingly given a second opportunity to strike.

## POLICY REVISIONS

Like changing technology, some forms of potential attacks might not have even been anticipated by those in charge of developing the original information governance policies. Corporate data policies are usually complex in nature and sometimes difficult to enforce. As a rule, organizations should work with their legal, compliance, and other departments in order to produce meaningful rules regarding how corporate data assets should be treated.[4]

Because the goal is to protect as much sensitive data as possible, information governance policies should regularly be reviewed in consultation with those in the organization that understand the threats. After doing so, the appropriate changes should be made to the policies so that they accurately reflect the current state of threats. For example, if an employee has taken their work laptop home and somewhere along the way ends up misplacing it or having it stolen, which in turn leads to the compromise of sensitive information, it may then be necessary to amend the company's information governance policies as it pertains to taking sensitive information outside of the office on laptops. The obvious work-around would be to permit company laptops to be taken home but prohibiting sensitive information from being saved to the hard drive. Instead, anyone needing sensitive information while at home or during travel would have to use a secure portal to access information stored and encrypted on the cloud. By doing so, the loss or theft of a company laptop will not jeopardize the organization's important information.

All too often, the initial creation of the information governance policies is viewed as a one-time job. Organizations forget to stay on top of their initial concerns, believing they will now be safe forever. To avoid this problem, companies need to be supportive of maintaining the originally established information governance committee and to empower the leader and those on the committee to be responsible for the policies' continual evolution.

According to Jim McGann in his publication entitled "Data assessments for center-wide information governance," the following are a few steps an organization can take in order to ensure their information governance policies remain relative:

- Emphasize the importance of information governance. Often it can be a means of job security.
- Make sure there is accountability to upper management so that tasks do not get pushed off to the side. The importance of the task needs to be emphasized. A lack of urgency or the failure to see governance as a necessary component can create cracks in efficiency.
- Schedule regular meetings to allow for updates or changes. Communication and transparency are important.
- Identify who has responsibility for each category/subcategory.
- Communicate to management and employees how continued maintenance is to the benefit of both the employer and the employee, and increases customer confidence.

- Keep personal and business information separate. The authors do not want employees to feel micromanaged. However, if employees recognize the importance of keeping their personal and business information separate, there is less chance of resentment.
- Create a checklist of what needs to be done, when, how often, and by whom. Each person assigned a task needs to be accountable to upper management.
- Keep the information simple, collecting only what is necessary and discarding what is not needed or outdated. This approach helps employees realize the benefit of reliable, easy-to-apply information.
- Use information governance as a secure tool rather than just a means of storage.
- Provide simple-to-use software that helps the user understand what data exist and where they are stored.
- Carry out periodic training and support for employees.
- Conduct periodic reviews to see if the information and the method by which it is obtain continues to contribute to the business.
- Make the continuous application and maintenance of information governance part of the job description.
- Management and owners need to take responsibility and apply the policies themselves. Employees will know they are expected to follow suit. Make it a habit.[5]

As McGann advises, the measures taken for information governance must also be continuously monitored for performance because of the ever-changing nature of risks that threaten businesses.[6]

As the information governance policies evolve and change, so will the need for additional training for employees. Policy manuals will have to be updated, and employees should be expected to sign new contracts each year reflecting that they understand the current policies. Signing should also be seen as an acknowledgment that they will do everything within their capacity to comply with policies in an effort to protect the company's proprietarily interests.

The following list of suggestions for achieving ongoing effectiveness in your organization's information governance policies is a good place to start when considering some of the essential steps:

## Evaluate Effectiveness of Information Governance Policies

- Consult the head of each department to determine if policies are working.
- Sample random employees.
- Determine if policies interfere with business productivity.
- Perform integrity testing by trusted sources (e.g., phishing scams, penetration tests).

- Foster clear communication between different branches of the organization.
- Evaluate whether security has been implemented in a fluid and non-intrusive manner.

## Encouraging Accountability and Ownership of Information Governance

- Social media (employees accountable for content)
- Rewards for positive actions
- Punishments up to termination for negative actions
- Programs for employee input
- Employee involvement on the information governance committee

## Training and Education of Employees About Information Governance

- Physical meetings
- E-mails to recap information governance policies
- Remind employees of the importance of these policies
- Positive reinforcement (i.e., rewards)
- Examples of companies that did not use information governance policies
- Updates for employees on changing policies
- Company culture becomes information based
- Posters
- Encouraging employees to remind co-workers of policies
- Employee quizzes
- Real-life examples communicated regularly
- Teaching an understanding of social engineering
- Annual and recurrent required training
- Covert testing of employees (nonpunitive)

Maintaining and keeping up-to-date with developments pertaining to a company's information governance programs and policies is as important as the initial establishment of these policies. Companies need to be proactive by examining what has been successful, encouraging accountability, deciding upon changes in the policies as necessary, and taking the steps to put updates into action. By doing so, companies can be assured that they have taken the most reasonable steps to protect their information, their clients, and their employees.

# References

1. Peters v. LifeLock Inc. et al., Arizona District Court case number 2:2014-CV-00576 filed March 20, 2014, U.S. District Court, Phoenix, Arizona.
2. Ibid.
3. Rand Corporation, "Black Markets for Hackers Are Increasingly Sophisticated, Specialized and Maturing," March 25, 2014, accessed February 2014. http://www.rand.org/news/press/2014/03/25.html.
4. Jim McGann, "Data Assessments for Center-Wide Information Governance," Data Center Journal, February 20, 2014, accessed February 2014. http://www.datacenterjournal.com/dcj-expert-blogs/data-assessments-centerwide-information-governance/
5. Ibid.
6. Ibid.

# Chapter 12

# Charting the Best Future Course for Your Organization

Knowing what to do and whom to call before, during, and after a data breach event can be the difference between success and failure, both for individual executives and the affected organization. This final chapter focuses on how information governance supports a data breach event with one primary recommendation: do not go it alone!

Data breach events do not discriminate. Whether your organization is a small or big business, a private or public company, a public/government entity, or a non-profit organization, complying with state and federal laws with privacy rules that differ from state to state will be one of the greatest challenges your organization will ever face. State and federal breach notification laws are new to most business executives, and the initial impulse is to give the information governance responsibility of a data breach to the information technology department.

This is a mistake, as most data breach events are more than IT and hacking drives. As the authors have indicated throughout this book, company insiders—such as current and former disgruntled employees and contractors—also drive data breach events. Company outsiders, including organized crime and cyberthieves, can also be the force behind data breach events. The scope and breadth of insider and outsider threats reach beyond technology and require a comprehensive review and the participation of every department within the organization.

Multiple groups and departments should be included in not just the development of the information governance policies and planning but also in the response to the data breach event. These groups—along with their related responsibilities and possible threats—comprise the following:

- Board of directors: needs to review and approve information governance police annually.
- Senior management: safeguarding employee and customer information has to be a priority.
- Information technology: needs to respond to hackers, malware and structural vulnerability.
- Human resources: includes current/former employee information; disgruntled current and former employees; and careless employees.
- Marketing/sales: includes current and former customer information; current/former disgruntled employees.
- Physical security: includes home office, multiple offices, remote offices, and equipment, including computers, laptop, cell phones, PDAs, etc.
- Finance, legal, and risk management: require a clear understanding of corporate responsibility and regulatory requirements (e.g., state breach notification laws, Red Flags Rule, HIPAA information security requirements, etc.).
- Vendor management: organizations need to understand their business relationships and the need for a formal due diligence process for every vendor or business partner based on the risk associated in doing business with each.

According to a SearchCIO article, "it wasn't that long ago that the topic of cyber crime was met with boredom by board members."[1] The fact is that cyber security and information governance is now a significant risk management issue with a new sense of urgency, from the boardroom to senior management to risk management. In addition, reputational risk, corporate branding, and marketing threats continue to challenge small and large businesses.

While the chief information or technology officer typically communicates with the board about the risk and costs of cybercrime and data breaches, information security and governance in general and data breach responses in particular need to be managed by the information governance committee overseen by the senior leadership team and board of directors.

According to the Ponemon Institute 2013 *Cost of a Data Breach Study*, the cost of a data breach in the United States was $188 per lost or stolen record.[2] The study examined the costs incurred by 277 companies in sixteen industry sectors after those companies experienced the loss or theft of protected personal data.[3] If you have a data breach that impacts 10,000 people, the costs are astronomical.

## Information Governance Impacts All Facets of an Organization

The impact of information governance falls on all divisions in a business. This impact can immediate and drastic, which is why the senior leadership—from the board of directors to the CEO—have to be strategic and visionary in creating and leading the information governance planning and response committees.

Based on the recommendation "not to go it alone," organizations should utilize outside help in the development and evolution of information governance programs. The use of external resources can be equated to utilizing a certified public accountant (CPA), which adds credibility to the organization's management team by having your financials audited, while reducing the risk of a material financial misstatement. An information governance consultant—like a CPA—will add credibility to the organization's management team by having your entire organization audited for gaps in information security, which can reduce the risk of a data breach event.

The following template from *Resources Magazine* recommends components of an information governance response plan to address a data breach event:

- Assess and treat risk. Addresses risk assessment, the process of identifying vulnerabilities, threats, and the probabilities of their occurrence and potential impact.
- Document information security policy. Outlines minimum standards for designing and updating an information security policy.
- Organize supporting structure. Describes the necessary components of the supporting structure within the organization as well as controls for customers, contractors, or partners, in order to sustain a successful information security program.
- Manage assets. Reviews guidelines for ownership, acceptable use, classification, labeling, and handling of assets, which marries the requirements of information security and privacy with disaster recovery.
- Retain trustworthy human resources personnel. Addresses the human resources components of information security, such as background checks, training, and disciplinary processes.
- Maintain physical and environmental security. Highlights characteristics to consider for protecting the organization's information security from physical and environmental threats, which may be accidental or malicious and includes acts of nature.
- Protect information technology communications and operations. Outlines the necessary security controls for information processing facilities, whether internal or external.
- Control information access. Examines aspects ranging from general policies covering access to specific issues such as password and timeout controls.

- Promote secure applications. Reviews the protection and verification procedures needed for all applications.
- Manage information security incidents. Covers the basics regarding incidents, prevention and lessons learned.
- Address business continuity. While most organizations have existing frameworks, this section specifically addresses the inclusion of information security in that process.
- Maintain the information security program. Describes necessary maintenance, including legal requirements, upgraded standards, and audit considerations.[4]

To be clear, information governance is more than an information technology related issue. Information security is a human resource (employee) issue. It is a marketing (communications) issue. It is a business development and account management (customer) issue. It is a physical plant (office) and remote office location issue.

## THE LESSONS OF HISTORY

A famous quote attributed to George Santayana says, "Those who cannot remember the past are condemned to repeat it."[5] But history rarely repeats itself exactly. There are always enough differences in the details that people do not learn anything from the past.

In a timeline covering 2005 to the present, the Privacy Rights Clearinghouse identified seven business sectors and tracked 4,214 data breaches affecting 864 million records through March 11, 2014, including the following: [6]

- Business, financial institutions/insurance services: 554 breaches affecting 258 million records.
- Business, retail: 497 breaches affecting 196 million records.
- Business, other: 547 breaches affecting 215 million records.
- Government: 676 breaches affecting 148 million records.
- Healthcare: 1,120 breaches affecting 30 million records.
- Education: 723 breaches affecting 15 million records.
- Non-profit: 97 breaches affecting 2 million records.

The breached data include employee and customer information, along with social security numbers that have been "lost or stolen" from some of the most well-known, financially strong, technology driven companies, universities, and organizations. Among these are Aetna Health Insurance, Bank of America, BlueCross/Blue Shield, Chase Bank, Citibank, Chevron, Duke University, Ernst & Young, Experian, Equifax, Facebook, General Electric, Fidelity Investments, Honeywell International, LinkedIn, Marriott International, McAfee, Notre Dame, Ohio State, Time Warner, T-Mobile, TransUnion, University of Texas, Verizon Communications, and Wells

Fargo.[7] One of the most overlooked trends relating to these data breaches is that approximately 30 percent of these events are hacking and IT related, while 70 percent of data breaches are related to social engineering and the human element.[8]

The Privacy Rights Clearinghouse also identified eight types of data breaches taking place on a regular basis:

- Unintended disclosure: sensitive information posted publicly on a website, mishandled, or sent to the wrong party via e-mail, fax, or mail.
- Hacking/malware: electronic entry by an outside party via hacking, malware, or spyware.
- Payment card fraud: fraud involving debit and credit cards that is accomplished through means other than hacking (e.g., skimming devices at point-of-service terminals).
- Insider: someone with legitimate access such as an employee or contractor intentionally breaches information.
- Physical loss: lost, discarded, or stolen non-electronic records, such as paper documents.
- Portable device: lost, discarded, or stolen laptops, PDAs, smartphones, portable memory devices, CDs, hard drives, data tapes, etc.
- Stationary device: lost, discarded, or stolen stationary electronic device such as a computer or server not designed for mobility.
- Unknown or other.

## THE LESSONS OF IDENTITY THEFT AND DATA BREACH

There are many lessons to be learned regarding identity theft and data breaches. In fact the lessons learned yesterday and today are not necessarily the lessons that will be learned tomorrow. Technology is changing rapidly, and as fast as we learn, new threats pop up. Some of the lessons that highlight this trend are below.

In October 2013, the *Silicon Valley Business Journal* published a news article on an Ernst & Young Survey entitled "Cybercrime: The Greatest Global Threat to Business Today."[9] This article highlighted four survey response points:

- 93 percent of companies maintained or increased their security budget over the last twelve months.
- 83 percent say current information security functions do not meet security needs.
- 31 percent reported a rise in security incidents of at least 5 percent over the past year.
- 14 percent of company budgets over the next year is earmarked for security innovation and emerging technologies.

As reported in a January 22, 2014, Help Net Security article, an independent study funded by GFI Software found that the workforce is acutely aware and worried about the threat to their personal online information.[10.] Additional findings included:

- Only 53 percent said their company had documented policies governing the use of company-owned IT devices and/or the use of computers in the workplace.
- 24 percent who do have documented policies in place admitted to violating them, further adding to concerns over IT security and safety for all employees.
- 7 percent admitted they have at some point lost a mobile computing device that contained company data.
- 87 percent admitted they felt at risk of becoming an identity theft victim while working at a small and medium-sized businesses (fewer than one hundred employees).

*InfoSecurity Magazine* determined that a lack of brand-equity damage control would stop customers from doing business if their personal data were compromised.[11] Additional findings about consumers included:

- 55 percent said that they would change banks.
- 39 percent said that they would get a new lawyer.
- 46 percent said that they would switch insurance companies.
- 42 percent would go to a different drug store/pharmacy.
- 40 percent would get a new doctor or dentist.
- 35 percent said that they would not return to their hospital.

On September 26, 2013, *SC Magazine* wrote an article entitled "Study: Uneasiness Concerning Insider Threats Grows for Security Professionals," where Advanced Persistent Threats are a major challenge that keep security professionals up at night.[12] The article goes on to highlight three points, including:

- Insider threats are increasingly becoming more difficult to thwart.
- Threats can be posed by a number of inside sources.
- 51 percent of respondents feared that "non-technical employees" with access to sensitive data posed the greatest risk.

### CONSUMER IDENTITY THEFT AND FRAUD

Identity theft and fraud stemming from the theft of data are the fastest growing crimes in our country. They are quickly becoming main foci for Federal law enforcement. Businesses are quickly picking up on the threat and addressing it accordingly. One specific type of threat that is becoming more prevalent is account takeovers. Criminals are stealing the credentials of individuals for use on eBay, Amazon, and other online sites to defraud not just the individual but the company itself. Once an individual has the stolen credentials, they are able to shop and order whatever they would like. When the consumer becomes aware of the fraudulent purchases, they have to spend time and effort to get the fraud rectified. When the company becomes aware, it often has to eat the cost of the items bought using the stolen credentials. It is expensive and time-consuming, and—as far as the criminal is concerned—it is anonymous and nearly fool-proof.

While one in three people received some notice of the possibility that they were the victim of identity theft, the business and financial world has made great strides at limiting the damage. One of the author's recently had his debit card copied without his knowledge and the perpetrators made a duplicate, fake card. The fraudulent card was only able to be used once as the bank was utilizing software that identified the activity as possibly fraudulent and shut off the card. The account had $750 withdrawn prior to fraud prevention kicking in, but the author was reimbursed. The bank, however, was still out the $750. The bank deserves credit for acting quickly and limiting the damage (not to mention rectifying the situation), but the fact remains that someone stole $750 from them. It is important to note that the number of actual incidents appears to be on the rise but actual losses appear to be shrinking due to the systems, policies, and procedures being implemented. Information governance plays an important role in avoiding theft in the first place and in limiting the damages once threats occur.

We must remember that identity fraud goes beyond the simple theft of debit or credit card numbers. The crime of stealing and fraudulently using stolen credentials is rising rapidly. A good information governance policy addresses that threat both from a customer standpoint (if they use credentials) and from an employee standpoint. Most companies have accounts set up with vendors and suppliers. The theft of their login credentials can lead to much more damage as the volume and dollar value can be much higher. Additionally, the accounts may not be watched as closely as personal accounts. Information governance will not necessarily address this issue. However, it should be noted and explained to those handling this function so they are alert and aware of the threat.

### *Prevention*

Any solid information governance program includes detection and reporting of issues as well as prevention. We also recommend teaching your employees some healthy data habits. Much like health insurance and preventative care lead to healthier employees who are more productive, so too helping an employee avoid becoming a victim of identity fraud or theft will help them to be a greater asset at work.

A few items for employees at home to consider:

- Track your accounts. Watch your accounts regularly, not just the balances but the transactions. If you are not sure of something that appears in your checking, savings, or credit account, contact the financial institution immediately.

- Keep your passwords and financial accounts secure. Use a safe or hidden spot at home, and use encryption on your phone, tablet and computer.
- Shred old documents.
- Use dual factor authentication if it is available. This means you will have to give verbal approval to access or use your account, which allows you to stop any unauthorized use.
- Request that your bank or other financial institution not use your social security number for verification. Most have the ability to use other information, so shutting off the most used way to access can stop data and identify thieves in their tracks.

These are great habits to have at home and in the workplace. The more your employees are aware of the threats and what to do about them the better.

## Detection

By monitoring accounts and looking for unusual activity, your business can limit exposure in the event of a hack or other breach that leads to identity or data theft. Information governance programs should always include detection protocols. Monitoring does not have to be just an internal program. There are services available that can assist in monitoring credit and accounts for unusual activity, and, as the example earlier showed, financial institutions are getting better at identifying when things don't appear right. It is a good idea to have a dialogue with your bank to make sure they are looking for issues and see if they have additional systems they can employ to help you.

## Resolution

Take any data breach notification seriously. If you are notified of a breach, take action. Generally, if you are notified of an incident the threat is very real and immediate. Most times the notification will come with some form of free monitoring. Take advantage of it, but keep your guard up and increase diligence. Be certain your policies spell out the actions necessary in the event of notification of a breach. A timely response can save you time and money, and can increase the likelihood of the fraudsters being caught.

The Federal Trade Commission released its February 2014 FTC *Consumer Sentinel Network Data Book*, wherein identity theft was cited as the top consumer complaints for the fourteenth consecutive year. American consumers reported losing over $1.6 billion to fraud overall in 2013.[13] The age group with the highest reported identity theft is 20–29, with 20 percent of complaints. Thirty-seven percent of all identity theft victims were 50 years of age or older.[14]

## STATE SECURITY BREACH NOTIFICATION LAWS

Forty-eight states, the District of Columbia, Guam, Puerto Rico, and the Virgin Islands have enacted legislation as of June 2014 requiring private or government entities to notify individuals of security breaches of information involving personally identifiable information. [15] These state laws commonly dictate who must adhere to the laws, define what is considered PII, lay out any notification requirements, and indicate whether compliance with Federal laws still suffice.

The following is a list of data breach laws in alphabetical order by state and US territories:

| State | Citation |
|---|---|
| Alaska | Alaska Stat. §45.48.010 *et seq.* |
| Arizona | Ariz. Rev. Stat. §44-7501 |
| Arkansas | Ark. Code §4-110-101 *et seq.* |
| California | Cal. Civ. Code §§1798.29, 1798.80 *et seq.* |
| Colorado | Colo. Rev. Stat. §6-1-716 |
| Connecticut | Conn. Gen Stat. §36a-701b |
| Delaware | Del. Code tit. 6, §12B-101 *et seq.* |
| Florida | Fla. Stat. §817.5681 |
| Georgia | Ga. Code §§10-1-910, -911, -912; §46-5-214 |
| Hawaii | Haw. Rev. Stat. §487N-1 *et seq.* |
| Idaho | Idaho Stat. §§28-51-104 to -107 |
| Illinois | 815 ILCS §§530/1 to 530/25 |
| Indiana | Ind. Code §§4-1-11 *et seq.*, 24-4.9 *et seq.* |
| Iowa | Iowa Code §§715C.1, 715C.2 |
| Kansas | Kan. Stat. §50-7a01 et seq. |
| Louisiana | La. Rev. Stat. §51:3071 *et seq.* |
| Maine | Me. Rev. Stat. tit. 10 §1347 *et seq.* |
| Maryland | Md. Code Com. Law §§14-3501 *et seq.,* Md. State Govt. Code §§10-1301 to -1308 |
| Massachusetts | Mass. Gen. Laws §93H-1 *et seq.* |
| Michigan | Mich. Comp. Laws §§445.63, 445.72 |
| Minnesota | Minn. Stat. §§325E.61, 325E.64 |
| Mississippi | Miss. Code §75-24-29 |
| Missouri | Mo. Rev. Stat. §407.1500 |
| Montana | Mont. Code §2-6-504, 30-14-1701 *et seq.* |
| Nebraska | Neb. Rev. Stat. §§87-801, -802, -803, -804, -805, -806, -807 |
| Nevada | Nev. Rev. Stat. §§ 603A.010 *et seq.*, 242.183 |

*(continued)*

## –Cont'd

| State | Citation |
|-------|----------|
| New Hampshire | N.H. Rev. Stat. §§359-C:19, -C:20, -C:21 |
| New Jersey | N.J. Stat. §56:8-163 |
| New York | N.Y. Gen. Bus. Law §899-aa, N.Y. State Tech. Law 208 |
| North Carolina | N.C. Gen. Stat §§75-61, 75-65 |
| North Dakota | N.D. Cent. Code §51-30-01 *et seq.* |
| Ohio | Ohio Rev. Code §§1347.12, 1349.19, 1349.191, 1349.192 |
| Oklahoma | Okla. Stat. §§74-3113.1, 24-161 to -166 |
| Oregon | Oregon Rev. Stat. §646A.600 *et seq.* |
| Pennsylvania | 73 Pa. Stat. §2301 *et seq.* |
| Rhode Island | R.I. Gen. Laws §11-49.2-1 *et seq.* |
| South Carolina | S.C. Code §39-1-90, 2013 H.B. 3248 |
| Tennessee | Tenn. Code §47-18-2107 |
| Texas | Tex. Bus. & Com. Code §§521.002, 521.053, Tex. Ed. Code §37.007(b)(5) |
| Utah | Utah Code §§ 13-44-101 *et seq.* |
| Vermont | Vt. Stat. tit. 9 §2430, 2435 |
| Virginia | Va. Code §18.2-186.6, §32.1-127.1:05 |
| Washington | Wash. Rev. Code §19.255.010, 42.56.590 |
| West Virginia | W.V. Code §§46A-2A-101 *et seq.* |
| Wisconsin | Wis. Stat. §134.98 |
| Wyoming | Wyo. Stat. §40-12-501 *et seq.* |
| District of Columbia | D.C. Code §28- 3851 *et seq.* |
| Guam | 9 GCA §48-10 *et seq.* |
| Puerto Rico | 10 Laws of Puerto Rico §4051 *et seq.* |
| Virgin Islands | V.I. Code tit. 14, §2208 |

The states with no security breach laws are Alabama, Kentucky, New Mexico, and South Dakota. In March 2014, a newly introduced data breach notification bill for New Mexico was sent to the state legislature. This bill would mandate that organizations notify breached individuals within ten days of breach discovery (unencrypted credit card data) and notify the state attorney general within ten business days if more than fifty New Mexico residents are affected.

## THE TARGET STORE DATA BREACH

The best known recent breach is the Target breach of late 2013. While the total cost is still up in the air and will not be known for years, suffice it to say it is well into the billions.

There are now class action suits being filed against Target and the vendors entrusted with getting and keeping them secure and compliant. When you consider the market share loss, the consumer confidence hit, the cost of reissuing cards, and the law suits, the damage is extreme. The press has been constantly reporting and updating the public for months, keeping the event in the forefront of consumer's minds.

A March 26, 2014, *US News & World Report* article by Tom Risen concerning the FTC investigation of the Target data breach states that the breach should be a warning to every business and organization in the United States.[16] "The Federal Trade Commission is investigating the data breach of retail giant Target that exposed millions of customers' personal information during the holiday shopping season, raising the possibility the company could face fines and ongoing regulatory scrutiny to prevent future lapses in security."[17]

The Federal government as well state governments around the country are looking more closely at how companies secure consumer data and how they react to suspected or actual events. The Target breach has been the impetus for much of the scrutiny, due to what is perceived as lagging security and missed opportunities to prevent the breach, according to a report published by the Senate Committee on Commerce, Science, and Transportation.[18] Testifying in late March 2014 during a hearing of that committee, FTC Chairwoman Edith Ramirez stated, "A company acts deceptively if it makes materially misleading statements or omissions."[19] "Further, a company engages in unfair acts or practices if its data security practices cause or are likely to cause substantial injury to consumers that is neither reasonably avoidable by consumers nor outweighed by countervailing benefits to consumers or to competition."[20]

During this hearing, the commission acknowledged the difficulty in preventing breaches and that "there is no one-size-fits-all data security program."[21] However, Senator John "Jay" Rockefeller, the chair of the committee, expressed his concern that companies are not doing everything they can to remedy the security concerns, stating "It is increasingly frustrating too that organizations are resisting the need to invest in their security systems. Target must be a clarion call to businesses, both large and small, that it's time to invest in some changes."[22] Rockefeller has introduced the Data Security and Breach Notification Act, which would require the FTC to issue security standards for Target and other companies that manage customer information,

## THE INSIDER THREAT

According to a survey of more than 200 organizations conducted by Deloitte Touche Tohmatsu, the primary security problem reported by IT auditors was excessive access.[23] The survey included participants across thirty-two countries from the top one hundred global financial institutions and banks and the top fifty global insurance companies.

Human error is the leading cause of IT system breaches, and most corporate security officials do not feel confident they can protect their organizations from internal cyberattacks.[24] In all, the survey found that the global recession is putting information at greater risk for these companies.

As was previously stated, Deloitte's security and privacy services practice found that 86 percent of survey respondents said human error is the leading cause of information systems failure.[25] This finding indicates that normally trustworthy employees can act abnormally during the stressful times of a poor economy. More than a 36 percent of the respondents expressed concern about insiders' misconduct, compared to only 13 percent who were concerned about external threats.[26]

## Closing Thoughts

Identity theft has evolved from a consumer fraud issue into a serious data breach threat where business reputations, marketing, branding, and finances are at risk. Businesses need to recognize current cyber and data breach trends and implement business practices to safeguard customer and employee personal information. Every business that fails to implement an information governance program will risk significant short- and long-term costs, including the trust and confidence of employees and customers.

In a way, computer servers are the new financial institutions. In light of this, every business and organization should be asking the following questions:

- What are your cyberassets worth?
- What are your current and former customer data worth?
- What are your current and former employee data worth?
- How secure are your current and former vendor relationships?
- How many current/former employees and vendors have had access to employee and customer data?
- What is the risk equation in signing up new business clients and taking on sensitive customer information?

Because business computer servers contain business data, employee data, and customer/member data, these computer servers are like financial institutions, where cyber and identity theft criminals target databases for profit.

So what can be done? As discussed throughout this book, every business should support its information governance program with annual updates and education, including steps to:

- Increase employee awareness of information governance programs and policies, including an employee education program in place to support said policies.
- Increase awareness of business data breach trends and consumer identity theft and fraud trends.
- Understand what type of customer and employee data are being collected and stored and how it is being secured, including the business policy for collecting and securing employee and customer data.
- Constantly assess and test your organization's needs and requirements by updating your company's information governance and best practices policies.
- Know your company's strengths and weaknesses by scheduling regular and comprehensive information security assessments.
- Implement baseline safeguards and controls.
- Be vigilant by updating and monitoring your company's safeguards and controls by utilizing information governance consultants to validate current safeguards and controls.
- Be aware of current and former employees and vendors by conducting background screening on current employees and vendors.

The concept of information governance will remain in the realm of business operations as long as companies are collecting and storing data. Likewise, information governance is now recognized as needing to be in the forefront of business operations. It can no longer be relegated to a few people in the organization's IT department. Further, the needs and policies of information governance will continue to grow and change. Like the threats that are ever evolving, information governance must also evolve to keep pace and maintain the security of sensitive data. It is a daunting task at times, but this task now belongs to everyone. The success of the future depends on the protective actions companies take today.

# References

1. Christina Torode, "Cybercrime is Now on the Minds of Board Members; senior CIOs, CISOs rejoice," *SearchCIO*, March 11, 2013, accessed March, 2014. http://searchcio.techtarget.com/news/2240179415/Cybercrime-is-on-the-minds-of-board-members-CIOs-CISOs-rejoice/.
2. Ponemon Institute, *2013 Cost of Data Breach Study: Global Analysis* (1.: Ponemon Institute, 2013), May, 2013; accessed March, 2014. http://www.ponemon.org/local/upload/file/2013%20Report%20GLOBAL%20CODB%20FINAL%205-2.pdf.
3. Ibid, p. 1.
4. Mark Pribish and Stacy Shields, "The Legal and Financial Liability of Identity Theft," *Resources Magazine* (Spring 2007), 34–35. http://issuu.com/tnaaustin/docs/spring07/.

5. George Santayana, *Reason in Common Sense*, vol. 1, C. Scribeners's and Sons, New York, (1905, accessed March, 2014), p. 284.

6. "Chronology of Data Breaches: Security Breaches 2005–Present," *Privacy Rights Clearinghouse*, modified December 31, 2013, accessed March, 2014. https://www.privacyrights.org/data-breach/.

7. Ibid.

8. Ibid.

9. "*Silicon Valley Business Journal*, http://www.ey.com/IE/en/Newsroom/News-releases/Press-release-2013—Cyber-crime—the-greatest-global-threat-to-business-today, Ernst and Young, December 12, 2013, accessed, March, 2014.

10. "Most SMB Employees in Fear of ID Theft in the Workplace," *Help Net Security*, January 22, 2014, accessed March, 2014. http://www.net-security.org/secworld.php?id=16245.

11. "Consumers Take Their Business Elsewhere After a Data Breach," *InfoSecurity Magazine*, October 22, 2013. http://www.infosecurity-magazine.com/view/35207/consumers-take-their-business-elsewhere-after-a-data-breach-/.

12. Jon Oltsik, The Enterprise Strategy Group, Inc., "The Ominous State of Insider Threats," September 26, 2013, http://www.vormetric.com/sites/default/files/ap_Vormetric-Insider_Threat_ESG_Research_Brief.pdf, accessed March, 2014.

13. Federal Trade Commission, *Consumer Sentinel Network Data Book for January–December 2013* (Federal Trade Commission, 2014), p. 3, accessed March, 2014. http://www.ftc.gov/system/files/documents/reports/consumer-sentinel-network-data-book-january-december-2013/sentinel-cy2013.pdf.

14. Ibid, p. 3.

15. National Conference of State Legislatures, January 26, 2014, http://www.ncsl.org/research/telecommunications-and-information-technology/security-breach-notification-laws.aspx.

16. "FTC Investigates Target Data Breach," *US News & World Report*, March 26, 2014, accessed March, 2014. http://www.usnews.com/news/articles/2014/03/26/ftc-investigates-target-data-breach/.

17. Ibid.

18. Ibid.

19. Ibid.

20. Ibid.

21. Ibid.

22. Ibid.

23. TMT Global Security Study, Deloitte Touche Tohmatsu, Ltd, 2013 http://www2.deloitte.com/content/dam/Deloitte/global/Documents/Technology-Media-Telecommunications/dttl_TMT_GlobalSecurityStudy_English_final_020113.pdf, accessed March 2014.

24. Ibid.

25. Ibid.

26. Ibid.

# Appendix A

## Information Security Personnel Check List

The following checklist can be used when selecting or recruiting someone to have responsibility over a company's network, infrastructure, data, and application security architecture, monitoring, and policy enforcement. The position may also oversee the creation and maintenance of information security policies, lead security risk assessment efforts, and own enterprise-wide awareness and security training development. This position should actively collaborate on the development of audit and governmental compliance practices and the implementation of systems.

- Be accountable for developing the overall information security vision, strategy and architecture for the enterprise, including policies and guidelines to support the vision and strategic direction.
- Ensure effective security and maintenance of the corporate databases and all of its institutions, including software and hardware within the corporation.
- Ensure applicable compliance with commercial, academic, legal, and other regulatory and legislative requirements in regards to information security, internal controls of systems, and networks. Establish procedures and standards necessary to control the IT environment; select and use appropriate test procedures and tools; and maintain an orderly system through which modifications may be made to existing systems.
- Maintain a high level of expertise on information security and other technology trends and best practices in technology, specifically in the information security arena.
- Provide day-to-day management of all information security governance activities, including: directing and analyzing enterprise-wide risk assessments, developing security policy, reporting security incidents, formulating security strategies/defenses, and managing the employee security education and training program.
- Oversee a network of security directors and vendors who safeguard the company's technology assets, intellectual property, and systems.
- Identify protection goals, objectives, and metrics consistent with a strategic information security plan.
- Manage the development and implementation of global information security policies, standards, guidelines, and procedures to ensure ongoing adherence to company's risk posture. Information protection responsibilities will include network

security architecture, network access and monitoring policies, and employee education and awareness.

- Work with other executives to prioritize governance and security initiatives and spending based on appropriate risk management and/or financial methods.
- Oversee incident response planning as well as the support of investigations into security breaches. Assist with disciplinary and legal matters associated with such breaches as necessary.
- Work with outside consultants as appropriate for independent information security audits.
- Be accountable for the organization's compliance with information security policies and corporate-wide compliance with state, federal, and international security mandates. Be accountable for appropriate legal, commercial, and academic regulatory requirements including FERPA and HIPAA.
- Draft an annual information security governance report for the executive committee and advise company leadership on emerging information security threats and evolving risks.
- Continuously monitor best practices to ensure the company is externally competitive and aligned with its internal business needs. Provide insight on trends and results to senior leaders as necessary.
- Actively engage and support the company's business continuity program and support the rapid pace of change across the enterprise.
- Oversee the execution of business continuity exercises in the technology, operations, and business areas.
- Ensure effective recruitment, development, performance, and retention of qualified and motivated staff to achieve objectives.
- Be an intelligent, articulate and persuasive leader who can serve as an effective member of the senior management team and who is able to communicate security-related concepts to a broad range of technical and non-technical staff.
- Build and maintain strong interpersonal relationships based on openness, transparency, and engagement. Communicate well with subordinates, peers, and superiors. Highly self-aware and recognized at creation and maintenance of highly functioning cross-organizational teams.
- In partnership with other divisions, create an IT security strategy/roadmap and an operating plan for optimal execution. Seek ways to add value and anticipate business needs.
- Build and nurture an integrated, energized and highly motivated information security team.
- Provide enabling support for the organization's international expansion.

Ten to fifteen years of progressive experience in computing and information security, enterprise risk management, evaluation and building of appropriate access and segregation of duties solutions, change management/control, SDLC, ERP, or major systems implementations, regulations/standards(PCI DSS, HIPAA, GLBA/FTC, etc.), compliance frameworks (ISO 27001/2, COBIT, SAS70/SSAE16), and global privacy standards.

At least seven years of managerial experience with demonstrated success in an executive leadership role

Must be an intelligent, articulate, and persuasive leader who can serve as an effective member of the senior management team and who is able to communicate security-related concepts to a broad range of technical and non-technical staff.

Must understand information security requirements and trends.

Possess experience with business continuity planning, auditing, and risk management, as well as contract and vendor negotiation.

Strong working knowledge of pertinent regulatory and statutory security requirements.

## Technical Aptitudes

- Strategic direction and vision.
- Ability to strike the right balance between risk and business agility.
- Strong relationship, management, communication, and presentation skills.
- Intellectual curiosity to ask the difficult questions to evolve the program.
- Ability to work easily with multiple internal and external partners, build consensus to implement. Ability to drive to reach closure, and manage expectations about delivery.
- Influence broadly and communicate clearly and frequently to ensure that key constituents understand the business requirements.
- A strong sense of urgency about solving problems, meeting challenging deadlines, and achieving critical goals.
- Establishes and maintains relationships internally and externally that are critical to the success of the business.
- Exercises intellectual honesty and influencing skills by identifying and presenting information or data in ways that are persuasive to others.
- Ability to effectively adapt to rapidly changing technology and apply it to business needs.
- Executes and delegates deliverables to ensure that timelines and results are achieved by holding self and others accountable.

- Strong knowledge and understanding of business needs, with the ability to establish and maintain a high level of customer trust and confidence in the security team's concern for customers.
- Certification in CISSP, CISA, and CISM.

## Leadership Skills

- Clearly assigns responsibility for tasks and decisions; sets clear objectives and measures; monitors process, progress, and results.
- Communicates a compelling and inspired vision or sense of core purpose; creates milestones and symbols to rally support behind the vision; makes the vision compelling and transparent across the enterprise.
- Accurately scopes out length and difficulty of tasks and projects; sets objectives and goals; breaks down work into the process steps; develops schedules and tasks/people assignments; anticipates and adjusts for problems and roadblocks; measures performance against goals.
- Clearly and comfortably delegates tasks and decisions; broadly shares responsibility and accountability; tends to trust people to perform; permits direct reports and others the ability to develop.
- Maintains and monitors employee engagement levels to drive a coordinated approach to enterprise objectives; drives a consistent approach and method to assist in clear messaging across the organization.

# Appendix B

| Threat | Consequences | Preventative Measures | Likelihood |
|---|---|---|---|
| Severe Storm | Flooding | ■ Vital Records and IS systems are above first floor.<br>■ Plastic bags are available to protect paper and magnetic tape.<br>■ Roof, windows, and outside doors are in excellent condition and have been tested for leakage.<br>■ Moisture sensors are located between real floor and raised floor.<br>■ Vital records and backup tapes are located offsite in a professional offsite storage facility. | Low to Moderate |
| | Power Outage | ■ Backup generator is on site and tested monthly.<br>■ Sufficient fuel is on site for backup generator.<br>■ Fuel supply vendors have been pre-contacted to deliver fuel.<br>■ Mobile backup generators have been pre-contacted for delivery. | Moderate |
| | Structural Damage | ■ Hot site/warm site is in place.<br>■ Telecommuting is available and supported.<br>■ Construction contractors have been contacted. | High |

# Appendix C

**Process Step or System Component**

**Potential failure mode**
(How could a failure occur?)

**Potential effect(s) of failure**
(What are the consequences of failure?)

**Severity**
(How severe would the impact be on a scale of 1 to 5?)

**Potential cause(s) of failure**
(What would be the cause of failure?)

**Occurrence**
(What is the probability of failure occurring on a scale of 1 to 5?)

**Current process controls**
(What controls are in place to detect or prevent failure?)

**Detection**
(What is the probability of failure being detected on a scale of 1 to 5?)

**Risk Point Number**
(Overall on a scale of 1 to 5)

# Works Cited

Antonopoulos, Andreas M. (May 31, 2011). *Can You Have Too Much Security?* Accessed February 4, 2014 http://www.networkworld.com/article/2177700/security/can-you-have-too-much-security-.html.

Behn, Robert D. (2003). Why Measure Performance? Different Purposes Require Different Measures. *Public Administration Review*, *63*(no. 5), 586–606. http://dx.doi.org/10.1111/1540-6210.00322.

Beveridge, Colin (October 2008). *The Better Practice Forum, Information Governance: Measures for Preserving Stakeholder Confidence.* http://www.eurim.org.uk/activities/ig/Measures_for_preserving_stakeholder_confidence.pdf.

Blair, Barclay T. (June 29, 2009). 8 Reasons Why Information Governance (IG) Makes Sense. *Association for Information and Image Management Blog.* http://aiim.typepad.com/aiim_blog/2009/06/8-reasons-why-information-governance-ig-makes-sense.html.

Bora, Kukil (August 3, 2011). McAfee Exposes Biggest-Ever Series of Cyber Attacks; Is China Responsible? *International Business Times.* November 8, 2013. http://www.ibtimes.com/mcafee-exposes-biggest-ever-series-cyber-attacks-china-responsible-821643/.

Chia, Terry (August 20, 2012). Confidentiality, Integrity, and Availability: The Three Components of the CIA Triad. *IT Security Community Blog.* http://security.blogoverflow.com/2012/08/confidentiality-integrity-availability-the-three-components-of-the-cia-triad/.

Comey, James B. (February 26, 2014). *"The FBI and the Private Sector: Closing the Gap in Cyber Security." Speech delivered at the RSA Cyber Security Conference.* San Francisco: California. http://www.fbi.gov/news/speeches/the-fbi-and-the-private-sector-closing-the-gap-in-cyber-security/.

Cowan, David (June 27, 2012). Comment: Too Much Security May Affect Business Practices. http://www.infosecurity-magazine.com/view/26550/comment-too-much-security-may-affect-business-processes/.

"Cyber Security: Software Threats." http://mediasmarts.ca/cyber-security/cyber-security-software-threats/.

Economist Intelligence Unit. (October 2008). *The Future of Enterprise Information Governance.* http://www.emc.com/collateral/analyst-reports/economist-intell-unit-info-goverence.pdf.

"Generally Accepted Privacy Principles." January 1, 2012. http://www.aicpa.org/interestareas/informationtechnology/resources/privacy/generallyacceptedprivacyprinciples/pages /default.aspx.

ISACA. (2009). An Introduction to the Business Model for Information Security. *Rolling Meadows, Ill.: ISACA.* http://www.isaca.org/Knowledge-Center/BMIS/Documents/IntrotoBMIS.pdf.

Leyden, John (August 29, 2012). Hack on Saudi Aramco Hit 30,000 Workstations, Oil Firm Admits. *The Register.* http://www.theregister.co.uk/2012/08/29/saudi_aramco_malware_attack_analysis/.

Logan, Debra (January 11, 2010). What is Information Governance? And Why is It So Hard? *The Gartner Blog Network.* http://blogs.gartner.com/debra_logan/2010/01 /11/what-is-information-governance-and-why-is-it-so-hard/.

Lowe, Jonathan (January 10, 2014). Can Existing Laws Protect Consumers After Target Breach? http://raycomgroup.worldnow.com/story/24421946/what-is-protecting-you-from-data-breaches/.

Manyika, James, & Roxburgh, Charles (October 2011). *The Great Transformer: The Impact of the Internet on Economic Growth and Prosperity.* McKinsey Global Institute. http://www.mckinsey.com/insights/high_tech_telecoms_internet/the_great _transformer/.

McGann, Jim (February 20, 2014). Data Assessments for Center-Wide Information Governance. *Data Center Journal.* http://www.datacenterjournal.com/dcj-expert-blogs/data-assessments-centerwide-information-governance/.

Moliere, Rudy, Isaacs, Leigh, & Lofton, Samantha (2013). Predictive Coding for Information Governance. 16–22. N.p: Iron Mountain Inc. In *Emerging Trends in Law Firm Information Governance.* http:// www.ironmountain.com/Knowledge-Center/Reference-Library/View-by-Document-Type/White-Papers-Briefs/P/Predictive-Coding-for-Information-Governance.aspx.

Ponemon Institute. (August 22, 2013). *Managing Cyber Security as a Business Risk: Cyber Insurance in the Digital Age.*

*Requirements Changing Rapidly, Market Success Relies on Hardware Expertise.* (February 27, 2013). http://www.nexcom.com/news/Detail/network-security-requirements-changing-rapidly-market-success-relies-on-hardware-expertise/.

Lillian Ablon, Martin C. Libicki, Andrea A. Golay. (March 24, 2014). *Markets for Cybercrime Tools and Stolen Data Hackers' Bazaar.* http://www.rand.org/pubs/ research_reports/RR610.html.

Rowe, Nathaniel (2012). *The Big Data Imperative: Why Information Governance Must be Addressed Now.* Boston: Mass: Aberdeen Group. http://aberdeen.com/Aberdeen-Library/8291/ RA-big-data-governance.aspx.

SAP Group. (December 2011). *Making Information Governance a Reality for Your Organization.* http://www.sapexecutivenetwork.com/files/Making_Information_Governance_a_Reality_for_Your_ Organization_(en).pdf.

Standards Australia. (2012). *The Value in Governance of Information Technology.* Sydney, Australia: Standards Australia Limited. http://www.standards.org.au/Documents/SA-Value-in-Governance-in-IT.pdf.

Stratford, Slemmons, Jean, & Stratford, Juri (1998). Data Protection and Privacy in the United States and Europe. *Iassist Quarterly, 22*(no. 3), 17–20.

Vesset, Dan., et al. (2012). *Worldwide Big Data Technology and Services, 2012–2015 Forecast, Vol. 1.* IDC: N.p.

Woods, Dan (December 12, 2013). How to Create A Moore's Law For Data. *Forbes.* http://www. forbes.com/sites/danwoods/2013/12/12/how-to-create-a-moores-law-for-data/2/.

- http://fbi.gov
- http://www.gartner.com
- http://www.intel.com (about Moore's Law).
- http://www.cnn.com (chap. 6, note 4).

# Index

Printed in the United States
By Bookmasters